SEX, L

CHA-

RELATIONSHIPS IN A

SING

CONFUSED CULTURE

LOVE

SEAN McDOWELL

B&H
PUBLISHING
NASHVILLE, TENNESSEE

978-1-0877-0729-7

Published by B&H Publishing Group
Nashville, Tennessee

Published in association with the literary agency
of Mark Sweeney & Associates, Naples, FL 34113

Dewey Decimal Classification: 152.4
Subject Heading: LOVE / GENEROSITY / INTERPERSONAL
RELATIONS

All Scripture quotations are taken from the English Standard
Version ESV® Text Edition: 2016. Copyright © 2001 by Crossway
Bibles, a publishing ministry of Good News Publishers.

Cover design by B&H Publishing.

2 3 4 5 6 7 8 • 25 24 23 22 21

I dedicate this book to my beautiful wife, Stephanie. You are not only my high school sweetheart, but you are still the love of my life and will be forever.

ACKNOWLEDGMENTS

There are many people to thank for a project of this sort. First, John Paul Basham for encouraging me to get me involved in this book project and the True Love Waits curriculum. I am grateful for the partnership and am truly honored you sought me out. It has been a blessing and joy to work with you! Thanks to Mark Sweeney, my agent and friend, for guiding me through the process. And some editors deserve a "shout out" for giving me great feedback: Amy Hall, Christopher Yuan, Preston Sprinkle, Taylor Combs, my wife (Stephanie), and my father (Josh).

And thanks to the students in my high school Bible class who gave me feedback on my first draft: Scott, Isabella, Faith, Aidan, Emma, Hazel, Dylen, Daniel, Rome, and Josh. It was fun to talk through many of these issues with you.

CONTENTS

Contents

PART 1

CHAPTER 1

The Invitation

The Matrix is one of my all-time favorite films. Even though I am a huge superhero fan and have watched many of the Marvel and DC movies over and over again, *The Matrix* is the only movie I have seen four times in the theater. That's right, *four times*.

You might be thinking, *this guy is crazy.* But as a young man fresh out of college, there was something about *The Matrix* that captured my imagination. Maybe you can think of a movie that has similarly captured yours.

In case you haven't seen it, the main character of the movie, Neo (played by Keanu Reeves), is a computer hacker who discovers that reality is not what he thinks it is. The world he believes is real is actually a computer simulation—the Matrix—that has been devised by artificially intelligent beings to distract humans as they use their bodies as an energy source. Neo discovers the truth, escapes from the Matrix, and joins a small band of humans in rebellion against the machines.

There are a lot of reasons to enjoy *The Matrix* as a movie. It's full of action and suspense, has a twist of romance, and has stunning visual effects (well, at least for its time!). Yet these are not the core reasons the movie captured me. Rather, it was because the movie raised *bigger* questions that made me reflect upon the trajectory of my own life, and in particular, my Christian faith. It made me consider what I was living *for*.

In the movie, Neo has a difficult choice to make: Will he choose the pleasures of the artificial world of the Matrix (the blue pill), or will he commit his life to truth, as costly and difficult as that may be (the red pill)? *The Matrix*, of course, is a movie, but in real life, each one of us faces a similar decision: *Will we choose a pleasure-centered life focused on self-fulfillment, or will we give our lives away for a greater cause?*

Jesus invites us to wrestle deeply with this question. In fact, He invites us to ask what we are *really* chasing in life. Good grades? Work? Success in sports? Marriage? Drama? Video games? You may care about some of these, or maybe all of them. But do they capture the depth of what you're *really* seeking? As good as these things can be, my suspicion is that, like Neo, you want your life to be about something *bigger*. You want your life to matter.

Jesus invites us to reorient the focus of our lives, to live for His kingdom instead of our own. In the Sermon on the Mount, Jesus said, "But seek first the kingdom of God and his righteousness, and all these things will be added to you" (Matt. 6:33). Jesus invites us to embrace a higher calling, living not for our own pleasures and goals but seeking *first* the things of God. Even though this road can be tough, and requires sacrifice, it is the most meaningful life we can live. According to Jesus, the God-focused life is the one that matters most. Through following Jesus, we experience God's "living water" rather than settling for a substitute (John 4:1–15).

So, what does it mean to seek first God's kingdom? In response to the question about the greatest commandment in the law, Jesus said to love God with all your heart, soul, mind, and strength, and love your neighbor as yourself (Mark 12:28–31). Simply put, the greatest commandment is to love God and love other people. Thus, if you want to seek God's kingdom first, you have to learn how to love God *and* love other people.

Thankfully, we can look to Jesus in this: "By this we know love, that he laid down his life for us, and we ought to lay down our lives for the brothers" (1 John 3:16). The way of love involves humbling ourselves in obedience to what God has called us to do. But Jesus isn't just our *model* of love. His death on the cross for our sins *enables* us to love. He makes us new creations—new people—who by the power of the Holy Spirit can give up things the world says we need for the sake of that which is truly life-giving—loving God and others. "We love because he first loved us" (1 John 4:19).

This is the great task God has for each one of us, and the Holy Spirit is ready to help us do it.

As a young college student, I remember being paralyzed with uncertainty about my career choice. I read a book by a former U.S. president, and he essentially said, "If you don't know what to do with your career, focus on how you can best love God and love other people." Simple, but profound.

Yet the contrast between the invitation of Jesus and the invitation of the world could not be starker. The world tells you to live for yourself; Jesus says to die to yourself. The world says to do whatever you want; Jesus says to cultivate the right wants. The world says to love yourself; Jesus says to love others as you love yourself.

The world disregards truth; Jesus claims that truth is found only through knowing and following Him.

Like Neo, you have a choice about the direction of your life. This isn't a choice you can put off until later. You're already making a choice whether you know it or not. We are all seeking some kingdom *now*, which is reflected in the ways we treat others *daily*. Here is the critical question Jesus is inviting you to consider: Will you view your whole life as a heroic adventure of walking faithfully in obedience to Him?

At this point, you might be wondering about the kind of book that you picked up. Isn't this a book about finding true love? After all, isn't the point of *chasing* something to *find* it? And doesn't happiness come from finding "real love"? Maybe you were expecting me to address LGBTQ issues and to answer popular questions like, "How far is too far?"

I will address both these topics, and many more. At the end of each chapter, I briefly address one tough, practical question like the following:

- *When am I ready to say, "I love you"?*
- *What should I do if someone is pressuring me for nude pictures of myself?*
- *Is masturbation okay?*
- *What should I do if a friend comes out to me?*
- *I am hurting from a past relationship. How long should I wait for another?*

But this is not primarily a how-to book on sex, love, and relationships. If that is the book you're looking for, you may need to look elsewhere. The point of this book is to motivate you to chase a bigger question, namely, "How do I seek God and His kingdom in my relationships with other people?" In other words, what does it mean to truly love God and love other people? If the question is framed this way, I think you will discover that you have the tools to work through the myriad of practical questions that arise in a romantic relationship, or as a single person aiming to honor God in your life and relationships.

Whether you get married someday or remain single, Jesus is inviting you to the great task of loving God and loving other people just as He loved us first. There are many ways to do this. In this book, we are going to focus on what it means to love God and others with our sexuality and in our relationships in the unique cultural moment that we find ourselves.

Are you ready? Let's go.

》》————→ **QUESTION** ←————《《
How do I stay sexually pure?

Begin by asking God for strength. Rely upon God for His strength rather than your own. Second, build convictions about *why* you are waiting. If necessary, go back through this book and discuss it with others. Third, find a good friend who shares your convictions about sex. Your friends will deeply shape your beliefs and behavior about sex. Fourth, be wise about media consumption. Protect your eyes and be careful about the movies, music, and social media you absorb. Fifth, avoid alcohol and drugs. Alcohol impairs judgment and makes decision-making tougher, which is why it often accompanies sexual activity.

CHAPTER 2

Who Will You Trust?

My first memory of my wife is in third grade (yes, I have *that* kind of story). We have now been married more than two decades and have three kids who are currently in high school, junior high, *and* elementary school. As you can imagine, our lives are busy and stressful at times, but they are also joy-filled and rich.

This past school year, my oldest son played varsity basketball as a freshman, and his team won the District 3 Championship. Watching him play this season was one of the great joys of my life. I was a gym-rat growing up and had the chance to play college basketball at Biola University, but I can truly say I have more fun watching my son play than I ever had playing basketball myself. While I can hardly believe that I'm writing this, it's true.

Why am I telling you this? The reason is that I love my kids dearly, and I try to demonstrate this to them through both my words and actions. As a result, they know they can trust me. They may not choose to always listen to me (after all, they're still growing up!), but they know I have their best interest at heart. Deep down, I know they believe I want the best for them, and as a result, they are willing to listen to me and to accept my discipline and instruction—although begrudgingly at times.

As a member of Generation Z, you have grown up with more voices speaking into your life than any previous generation. And the reason is simple—smartphones. You have *far* more people speaking into your life than your parents or grandparents ever had at your age. This raises a number of issues, but none more vital than the question: *Who will you trust?*

Who will you listen to? Politicians? The news? Social media influencers? Teachers? Friends? Religious leaders? Who are the voices you trust to help you navigate reality?

How you answer this question influences *every* decision you make. And this is especially true in the area of sexuality and relationships. Quite obviously, our world is filled with messages contrary to Scripture. Music. Movies. Social media. And so on. Digital technology is a wonderful tool for learning and connecting with others (I love my smartphone!), but it also allows endless voices, some subtle and others more overt, to persistently speak messages into our lives about sex, love, and relationships. Again, who will you trust?

As I mentioned earlier, my kids trust me because I am older, wiser, but more significantly, they know I love them. If they couldn't trust that I had their best interests in mind, my age and wisdom would mean nothing to them.

Yet even as much as they trust me, I am still an *imperfect* father. I try to honor God as a husband and father, but I fall short all the time.

In contrast, God is a *perfect* heavenly Father. He not only knows everything and has unlimited power, but He loves us more deeply than we can even grasp.

The greatest act of love God has shown us was the death of Jesus. Jesus said the greatest act of love is to lay down your life for another (John 15:13). Sacrificing your life is the highest act of love because your life is the most valuable thing you have to give. I love my kids, and thus would gladly lay down my life for them.

Would I die for an enemy? That's a tougher question. Yet that's exactly what Jesus did for us.

Paul writes, "But God shows his love for us in that while we were still sinners, Christ died for us" (Rom. 5:8).

Jesus did not have the precondition that we repent *before* He laid down His life. He did not die for good people. He died for sinners. God loves us not because of anything we did, but because of who He is. God paid the ultimate price, through the death of His Son, so we could have eternal life.

Will you trust *this* God?

In the garden of Eden, Satan tempted Adam and Eve, the first humans, by trying to undermine their confidence in the character of God. He wanted to sow seeds of doubt in their minds and hearts about God. Did God *really* have their best interests in mind, or was He keeping them from something better? After all, the fruit they weren't supposed to eat looked tasty to the senses, striking to the eyes, and appealing to the mind (Gen. 3:6). If God were good, would He *really* keep something so attractive from them?

Adam and Eve listened to the crafty prompting of Satan. They ultimately lost confidence in the goodness of God, and thus ate the fruit. Sadly, they came to doubt the character of God, and while they may have *believed* their choice was wise, their disobedience brought immeasurable suffering into the world.

Aren't we faced with the same kind of choice today? The world offers "fruit" that looks pleasurable, fun, and satisfying. It is as if Satan were saying, "Did God *really* say sexual activity was only for marriage? Is sexual activity *really* that big of a deal? Does porn *really* hurt anyone? As long as sex is consensual, there's nothing wrong with it, right? Are you really going to judge someone else for how they love? Why embrace a view of sex, love, and gender that seems so closed-minded? Isn't the Christian sexual ethic unrealistic today anyway? *Isn't God holding out on you?*"

These voices can be powerful and convincing, especially since we hear them incessantly through social media, school, television, celebrities, and so on. As a result, we are tempted to stop taking God at His Word and wonder, "Did God *really* say . . . ?"

Yet Jesus invites us to something greater. He invites you to reject the counterfeit pleasures of this world, and to focus your life on loving God and loving other people. While the reward is far greater, it comes as a sacrifice in the present.

I would be dishonest if I didn't ask you to count the cost up front, so here it goes: Are you prepared to sacrifice certain worldly pleasures for the sake of faithfulness to Christ? Are you willing to give up some things our culture says are *good* in order to do what God says is *best*? As Jesus said, "Whoever loses his life for my sake will find it" (Matt. 10:39).

Personally, I believe we can and should trust God, because I am convinced God is good—for

Are you willing to give up some things our culture says are *good* in order to do what God says is *best*?

a number of reasons. I'll mention just two here. First, Scripture teaches it. King David wrote, "Oh give thanks to the LORD, for he is good, for his steadfast love endures forever!" (Ps. 107:1). God doesn't merely *do* good things; He *is* good.

Second, Jesus reveals the good character of God through His miraculous healings, profound teachings, death on the cross, and resurrection from the dead. The life, death, and resurrection of Jesus demonstrate that God is truly good and that He has not abandoned this world to chaos or wickedness. God is in control and working all things together for the good, and the "good" He's working toward in our lives is to make us like Christ (Rom. 8:28–29).

Why is this so important? Think about it: How you understand the character of God shapes how you evaluate His commands. If you don't truly believe God is good, you'll tend to view His commands as oppressive and controlling. You'll be tempted to consider God a "cosmic killjoy," intent upon stealing your fun. On the other hand, believing God is good sets you free to trust Him and His plan as the best path to both giving and receiving genuine love. Loving this good God motivates obedience to Him.

Still, I can't promise you the journey will be easy. In fact, it will likely be harder than following the ways of the world—at least in the short run. After all, isn't it easier to give in to sin than to resist it? Wouldn't it be easier to adopt the cultural understanding of sex and gender than to stand in patient and loving biblical *opposition*? Yes, of course it would. Yet in this book, I want to encourage you to consider the value of doing things that are difficult. Difficult things are meaningful. Nothing worth having comes easy.

If you follow Jesus, there will inevitably be times you wonder whether the sacrifice is worth it. In his letter *Saved in Hope*,

Pope Benedict XVI said that "the present, even if it is arduous, can be lived and accepted if it leads toward a goal, if we can be sure of this goal, and if the goal is great enough to justify the effort of the journey."[1] Living for God is the greatest goal we can embrace. He is the only goal worth giving our entire lives to. While the road is not easy, we do know where it leads in the end—to eternal life. Our present sufferings pale in comparison to the glory that awaits us (see Rom. 8:18–25).

Regardless of what our culture proclaims, if you are a follower of Jesus, you are *always* on the right side of history.

Even though I am an *imperfect* father, my kids trust me, because I am older, wiser, and love them deeply. How much more should we trust our *perfect* heavenly Father who not only knows everything, and has unlimited power, but loves us more profoundly than we can ever fully comprehend?

Our journey toward loving people begins by trusting that God is good, and by committing to Him and following *His* plan for our sexuality, rather than embracing everything our culture tells us.

Let's dive in.

---

[1] Pope Benedict XVI, *Spe Salvi*, 1 (Boston: Pauline Books and Media, 2007).

>>————————→ **QUESTION** ←————————《
When is the right age to date?

First, obey your parents. Whether you agree with them or not, your primary job is to honor your parents by respecting their standards. To me, the right age to date is *when you are mature enough to handle the emotional (and sexual) pressures that can accompany a date.* This might be at seventeen or twenty-two. Although I personally think sixteen should be the earliest, the key issue is the level of maturity. Start with these questions: Can you set and keep healthy sexual standards? Can you treat a date with respect? Do adults in your life think you are ready?

CHAPTER 3

The Sexual Ethic of Jesus

Have you ever imagined what the world would be like if everyone lived the sexual ethic of Jesus? Would the world be better or worse?

Not long ago, I had the chance to have a public conversation on the Bible and homosexuality with Matthew Vines, author of *God and the Gay Christian*. Matthew believes that Scripture only condemns certain kinds of same-sex relationships, but permits the kinds of mutual and monogamous same-sex relationships we see today. In contrast, I believe Scripture clearly teaches that sex is reserved for the permanent marital union of one man and one woman.

Matthew won the coin toss, yet he chose to allow me to speak first. The goal of my opening speech was not only to articulate the historic Christian view of sex and marriage, but also to show the goodness *and* beauty of this position. In other words, my hope was to demonstrate that the world would truly be a better place if everyone lived the sexual ethic of Jesus. After all, "all things were created through him and for him" (Col. 1:16).

So, how did I aim to accomplish this? Consider a brief excerpt from my opening speech:

> Imagine a world in which everyone followed God's design for sex and marriage: There would be no sexually transmitted diseases. No abortions. No brokenness from divorce. Every child would have a mother and a father and experience the love and acceptance each parent uniquely offers. There would be no rape, no sex abuse, no sex trafficking, no pornography, and no need for a #MeToo campaign. Think of the healing and wholeness if people simply lived Jesus' life-giving words regarding human sexuality.[1]

Can you imagine such a world? Isn't it good *and* beautiful? Following the sexual ethic of Jesus would quite literally transform our world for the better:

- There would be no victims or users of pornography.
- There would be no sexual exploitation, sexual trafficking, or sexual abuse.

---

[1] To see my discussion with Matthew, check out, "What Does the Bible Say about Homosexuality?" on YouTube: https://www.youtube.com/watch?v=yFY4VtCWgyI. And to read my opening speech, check out, "The Opening Speech from My Conversation with Matthew Vines," https://seanmcdowell.org/blog/the-opening-speech-from-my-conversation-with-matthew-vines (Feb 1, 2018).

- There would be no sexually transmitted diseases.[2]
- There would be no rape.
- There would be no pregnancies outside of a loving, committed marriage.
- There would be no crude, degrading sexual humor.
- There would be no abortions, because even an unplanned-for child would be loved and cared for by his or her parents.
- There would be no pain from divorce.
- There would be no deadbeat dads.
- There would be no prostitution.
- There would be no men who leave their wives for younger women.
- There would be no adultery or the devastation it brings to families.

Wouldn't such a world be far better than our own? Of course!

In the last chapter, we saw that Satan aims to call into question the character of God. Why? Because we evaluate God's commands in light of how we view His character. Scripture teaches that *God is good*; thus, we can trust His commands. Yet in this chapter, we need

---

[2] Technically, a sexually transmitted infection (STI) is different than a sexually transmitted disease (STD). An individual with an STI has an infection, but it has not yet developed into a disease. An infection is the first step of a disease, which begins when a virus or bacteria enters the body and begins multiplying. All STDs begin as STIs. See Nick Corlis, "STI vs. STD," STDcheck.com blog (June 23, 2015); https://www.stdcheck.com/blog/std -vs-sti-whats-the-difference/. I use both terms throughout this book.

to go a step further. Not only is God good (as we have seen), but *His commands are intended for our good.*

God's commands are not random, inconsistent, or meaningless; they stem from His character and are intended to help human beings flourish in their lives and relationships.

The biblical writers understood this point, even though they often failed to live it. King David said, "The law of the LORD is perfect, reviving the soul; the testimony of the LORD is sure, making wise the simple" (Ps. 19:7). In his final speech before the Israelites entered the promised land, Moses told the Israelites that God desired they walk in obedience to His commands, which *were for their own good* (Deut. 10:12–13).

We may not fully understand God's commands—just like children don't fully understand the good directive their parents often give them. But *His commands are always for the good of both societies and individuals.*

You might be thinking, *Wait a minute, are you saying there is real right and wrong that everyone is supposed to follow?* Yes, that is *exactly* my point. And if you reflect upon it for a moment, I think you will agree.

Consider a few scenarios: Would it be okay if a group of guys decided to take advantage of a girl who couldn't defend herself? Is it morally permissible to take advantage of someone sexually when they are drunk? Of course not.

You know that honesty is good. You know that terrorism is wrong. You know that unselfishness is right. You know that stealing is wrong. Even if someone said that rape was okay, you know deep down in your heart that it is wrong to violate another human being in this horrific manner. You know this is wrong not because of what society says, but because of the nature of both human beings and the violent, abusive nature of rape.

Yet how do we *know* these things? The apostle Paul says that God has placed right and wrong on the human heart (Rom. 2:14–16). In other words, you know right and wrong because you are a moral being living in a moral universe.

But what if people disagree with you? Does that make moral truth relative? No!

C. S. Lewis famously noted how belief in objective right and wrong is inescapable: "Whenever you find a man who says he does not believe in a real Right and Wrong, you will find the same man going back on this a moment later. He may break his promise to you, but if you try breaking one to him, he will be complaining 'It's not fair' before you can say Jack Robinson."[3]

A few years ago, I moderated a debate between my Christian high school students and some agnostic and atheist students from the local public school. One of my students argued that the existence of a universal moral law, which we all inherently know, points to the existence of a Moral Lawgiver, namely God. In response, one of the agnostic students claimed that morality is subjective and thus does not point to the existence of God. In fact, he compared morality to choosing an ice cream flavor and said it is all a matter of taste.

But then during his closing statement, the same agnostic student blasted the (primarily Christian) audience for being bigoted, hateful, and homophobic. Do you notice something strange? Do you notice the inconsistency? He *first* claimed that morality was

---

[3] C. S. Lewis, *Mere Christianity* (New York, NY: Macmillan, 1960), 19–20.

subjective like ice cream, and then moments later, without even realizing it, denounced Christians for being immoral.

C. S. Lewis was correct: right and wrong are inescapable. We live in a moral universe, and we all know it.

Just as God is the source of the physical laws of the universe, He is also the source of its moral laws. The world operates according to physical laws, which humans discover, and it also operates according to moral laws, which are written on the human heart. Philosopher Peter Kreeft put it this way, "The law of gravity is true because that's the *nature* of matter. The law of love is true because that's the *nature* of man: man was *designed* to love, as matter was designed to attract."[4]

Living the sexual ethic of Jesus brings true human flourishing. And the reason is simple: following Jesus puts us in touch with reality. There is a physical reality *and* a spiritual reality, and it is only when we align our lives with both that we can be truly free.

Let's unpack this more in the next chapter.

---

[4] Peter Kreeft, *Making Choices: Finding Black and White in a World of Grays* (Cincinnati, OH: Servant Books, 1990), 45.

》》————————→ **QUESTION** ←————————《《
When am I ready to say, "I love you"?

The words "I love you" are perhaps the most powerful three words in the English language. We must be wise when using them. Simply put, you are ready to say "I love you" *when you truly love someone.* How do you know when you love someone? As you may recall, love is not a feeling, but a commitment to seek the best for another. If you truly love someone, you will focus on protecting and providing for their spiritual, physical, and relational growth. Love is not self-focused but is focused on the best for the other. When this happens, you may be ready to say, "I love you."

CHAPTER 4

Experiencing True Freedom

How would you define what it means to be truly free? I don't mean the kind we talk about when we say the United States is "the land of the free." I simply mean, as a human being, *what does it mean to be free?*

Recently I asked a group of high school students this same question. After some discussion and reflection, they agreed on the following definition: "Freedom is being able to do what you want without restraint." In other words, the free person does whatever he or she wants without any person or law hindering them.

There are two parts to this definition that we need to explore. The first is being able to do what you *want*. Is the person who does what she wants necessarily free? I am not sure she is.

As a college student, I had the chance to work at a T-shirt stand at the 1996 Olympics in Atlanta, Georgia. One of my coworkers was an alcoholic, and he couldn't make it through a day without multiple drinks. Although we never discussed religion, he knew I was a Christian, and thus he said to me out of the blue, "You know,

I can drink if I want." I simply replied, "I agree you are free to drink if you want. But I have a question for you. Are you free *not* to drink?"

My point was simple: he was only free to drink if he could choose *not* to drink. In reality, he was a slave to his "passions and pleasures," as Paul describes in Titus 3:3.

The free person is the one who can say "no" to the bottle. The free person is the one who is able to say "no" to looking at porn. The free person is the one who says "yes" to loving God and loving other people *as they were meant to be loved*. Thus, freedom is not being able to do whatever you want, but cultivating the right wants that allow you to properly love God and other people. Look, if freedom is doing whatever we want, *then no person is actually free*. People can't fly, see through walls, or walk on water no matter how much they want. If this is what freedom is, no one is free.

What about the second part of the definition? Is freedom doing what you want *without restraint*? Again, I am not sure that it is. Think about it: Are you freer if you bang on piano keys without restraint, or if you follow the guidance of an instructor who disciplines and guides you? The answer is obvious. The instructor helps restrain your actions so you can use a piano as it was meant to be used. Discipline and restraint are necessary for producing beautiful music.

Paradoxically, freedom comes not from resisting restraint, but from submitting to the right restraint.

This is why boundaries are necessary for true freedom. Psalm 119:9–10 asks, "How can a young man keep his way pure? By guarding it according to your word. With my whole heart I seek you; let me not wander from your commandments!" In other words, seeking God and following His commandments are the best ways a young man (or young woman) can stay pure. The psalm also discusses how living *without* boundaries enslaves us to the hunger of greed. Paradoxically, throwing off God's commandments actually restrains our freedom.

According to the Christian worldview, true freedom is not a matter of doing what you want without restraint, but cultivating the *right* wants and living in obedience to God's will. In other words, freedom results when our wants align with the will of God. Adam and Eve sinned because they followed a false freedom. Satan told them that God wasn't good, and tricked them into believing they would be freer if they threw off restraints, but the result was death and suffering. They failed to see that freedom comes through following God and His Word.

Does that mean freedom comes through gritting your teeth and simply choosing to do what is right? No! If you try to be obedient through your own effort, you will inevitably fail. In fact, if you try to follow God's commands in your own power, you will fail *miserably*. Trust me, I've been there. The Christian worldview uniquely teaches that we are incapable of living a good life in our own power. Sin has rocked us to the core (Rom. 3:9–20).

The secret to the Christian life (and what separates Christianity from other faiths) is found in the scandal of grace. It is when we acknowledge our own brokenness and inability to live as God wants us to that we can begin to experience inner transformation.

After describing his persecutions and shortcoming, the apostle Paul said, "For when I am weak, then I am strong" (2 Cor. 12:10). In other words, Paul knew that the power of the Christian life comes when we rely upon the power of Christ to work through us. Our strength comes in acknowledging our weakness and failure and depending upon God.

This is why what we call "spiritual disciplines" are so important. Just as freedom comes to a piano player who practices on a regular basis, freedom comes to the Christian who "practices" the spiritual life. Spiritual disciplines such as prayer, Scripture reading, tithing, confession, fasting, worship, and fellowship are vital for cultivating the kind of character in which our wants align with the will of God.

Back to the original question I asked the students—*What does it mean to be free?* Once they gave me their initial definition, I followed up with a second question: "If a personal God exists, would that change how we understand freedom?" After some reflection and interaction, they agreed that the nature of freedom would essentially be the same (doing what you want without restraint), but that God adds *consequences*. God may add guilt in this life, or judgment in the next, but according to these students, His existence would make no significant difference as to what it means to be a person who is free, other than the consequences that result from our choices.

What these students failed to understand is that the existence of a personal God changes everything. That's right, *everything*. Although their definition needed some adjustment, the students rightly understood that part of freedom is having the capacity to make choices for our own lives. They understood *freedom from*—being able to make choices that are not coerced by another. God gave us freedom in the first place in the garden (Gen. 2). This sense of freedom is often considered the "negative" sense of freedom. But it is only half the story.

If God exists, then we also need to consider a positive aspect, which is sometimes called "positive" freedom, or *freedom for*. In other words, we are truly free when we are free for something—namely, for fulfilling our purpose. This leads us to ask the all-important question, *What is our purpose?*

The first thing we learn about God in the Bible is that God is the Creator: "In the beginning God *created* . . ." (Gen. 1:1a). The world is not a cosmic accident but is purposefully fashioned by a Creator. Since He is the Creator, He is the Designer. He is the great Purpose Giver to all He has created.

Just like a car that has been designed by its creator to operate in a certain fashion, and is only "free" when used accordingly, humans have also been created *for* a greater purpose and experience freedom when they discover and live *that* purpose. The free person not only has the capacity of choice (freedom *from*) but orients his or her life to God's design (freedom *for*).

What has God made us *for*? A student once told me that the freest person would live alone on an island so no one could constrain his or her choices. While such a person might be free in the negative sense, this individual would not be truly free in the positive sense. Why? Because Scripture reveals that God has made us *for* relationship with Him *and* with others. Jesus said the greatest commandments are to love God and love others (Mark 12). Thus, we cannot be free in isolation, but only in healthy, intimate relationships with both God and other people.

As we will see in the next chapter, it is only in committed relationships with other people, in accordance with God's design, that we experience the truly free and "abundant" life Jesus offers us.

»————→ QUESTION ←————«

How do I deal with someone pressuring me to have sex?

Recently, a student of mine asked me this question, so I asked her if she believed that he loved her. After some thought, she came back to me and said no. She realized he pressured her because he was focused on what he wanted, not on what was best for her, and that his pressure was a form of sexual abuse. Since she did not want to be used by him, she broke off the relationship. She did two things right. First, she asked a leader for guidance and support. Second, she broke off the unhealthy relationship because she knew she deserved better. If pressured sexually, I hope you will follow her lead.

CHAPTER 5

The Freedom of Commitment

While my grandfather remembered the attack on Pearl Harbor, and my mom remembers the Kennedy assassination, I was born after these events and thus have no memory of them. But I will *never* forget the tragic events of September 11, 2001, just as you will never forget the COVID-19 pandemic. I woke up early on 9/11 and turned on the television to catch the news before heading to class. One of the Twin Towers was on fire because it had been hit by a plane. In a short amount of time, the other tower was hit, and eventually they both collapsed, resulting in the deaths of nearly three thousand people. This memory is forever etched into my heart and mind.

For the next few weeks, my wife and I tearfully watched the news coverage night after night. Our hearts broke for the husbands who lost their wives, the children who would grow up without fathers, and the friendships that abruptly came to an end. Like everyone else, we grieved that so many people needlessly lost their lives.

But we did not grieve for the buildings. Sure, we may regret how the New York skyline has changed with the loss of the Twin Towers, but we did not grieve the destruction of the buildings as we grieved the loss of lives.

Why am I bringing up such tragic events in a book on relationships? The answer is quite simple: *tragedy reveals what we value most*.[1] When the passengers on Flight 93 discovered that their plane was hijacked, they instantly called their friends and family to express their love and to say goodbye. No one made a call to check their bank account, or to find out the final score of a sporting event. They all called to connect one last time with their loved ones for one simple reason: *relationships matter most*. And we all know this when we take the time to reflect on it. In fact, you know this first-hand because of the quarantine from the COVID-19 pandemic. Wasn't the hardest part being away from your friends? Didn't you yearn to be with them? More than anything, my kids told me they missed being with their classmates, teammates, and friends. My guess is that the same was true for you.

This same truth can be seen in movies. Take the Marvel film *End Game*. While the Avengers struggle mightily to defeat Thanos, the movie is compelling because it is about characters we care about and can relate to. We root for Captain America to get one last dance with Peggy. We root for Hawkeye to be reunited with his family. And we root for Iron Man to become the husband and father for his family, as well as a mentor (to Spider-Man) that he yearns to be.

---

[1] Credit to my colleague and friend Gregory Ganssle for this insight. See his book *Our Deepest Desires: How the Christian Story Fulfills Human Aspirations* (Downers Grove, IL: InterVarsity Press, 2017), 21–32.

Great movies are about human drama and relationship. The *Rocky* movies are not just about boxing, but about the relationship between Rocky and his wife, son, friends, and his mentee, Adonis Creed. The classic film *Titanic* was so popular not because it was about a sinking ship, but because people resonated with the love story between Jack and Rose.

Scripture teaches that God made human beings for relationships with Him *and* with other people. Adam walked with God in the garden of Eden. He had perfect health, a perfect environment, and could work and play with the animals, and yet God declared that it was not good for Adam to be *alone* (Gen. 2:18). Why? The first reason is because God gave humans the task of multiplying and filling the earth (Gen. 1:28), and Adam could not do this without Eve. But second, God also made humans to be in relationship with other human beings. We are not meant to live in isolation. We are made to live in families and communities with other people.

We can only be free through commitment and faithfulness.

Thus, since we are made for relationships, we can only be free through commitment and faithfulness. This may strike you as backwards! After all, we live in a world of endless options. From consumer products, to music, to streaming television, you can seemingly have *what* you want, *when* you want it, *how* you want it, and with *whomever* you want. So, in terms of marriage, why commit to one person for life? Why limit yourself?

I live in Orange County, and it often seems people have little commitment to anything. People switch schools, sports clubs, and churches with barely a second thought. The philosophy seems to be: *if you find something better, take it.*

Having options can be good, but when there are unlimited options, people become less willing to work through conflict—especially in something as important as a marriage or relationship. After all, there might be someone better out there.

As I mentioned earlier, my wife and I have been married more than two decades. I love her dearly and cherish our relationship. Yet there have certainly been times of frustration, conflict, and disagreement where it *felt* as if it would be easier to walk away. Yet no matter how I may *feel*, walking away is not an option. I meant my vows when I first gave them, and I stick by them today. And so does my wife. Our commitment to each other gives us the confidence—and *freedom*—to know that we can and will work through difficulties. Commitment helps us transcend conflict.

The value of commitment is also true in the dimension of sex. Our world proclaims endless options as the path to sexual freedom. But in reality, sex is actually most satisfying when there is trust, love, and commitment. In a committed, loving relationship partners don't have to be anxious about sexual performance, worried about comparison, or concerned about contracting a sexually transmitted infection (STI). Instead, married couples are *free* to experience the joy of sex as God designed it.

But if sex requires the commitment of marriage, what about singles? If they can't have sex, how can they possibly be free?

A single person who wants to honor the Lord will not be sexually active. But singleness offers a different kind of freedom than marriage. In fact, the apostle Paul says it is good to be single! He even wished others would be single like him (1 Cor. 7:7–8).

What freedoms do single people have that married people don't? For one, they are free from the definitions and expectations culture forces on them about sex and relationship. Second, married people are anxious about pleasing each other, says Paul, but singles can be free to focus on serving the Lord and loving other people.

A young single man named Roberto likes to compare himself to Gandalf.[2] Why? He said, "I am not married, so I do not need to stay in one place. So, God can send me wherever He needs me to go." Rather than seeing his singleness as a curse, he sees it as a blessing. Like Paul, he views being single as a kind of freedom rather than a restriction. Thus, he finds his joy in loving and serving others.

The point is not that singleness is easy. It's not. Neither is marriage. The point is that God invites us to embrace a different kind of freedom than the kind offered by the world. God invites each one of us—whether male or female, single or married—to the freedom that comes from committing our lives to loving other people *in* relationship. This is the only path to experiencing the truly rich life Jesus proclaimed.

Given that Jesus invites us to love people, it is vital we properly understand the nature of love. That's the topic of the next chapter.

---

[2] See Joseph Prever, "The Curse of the Ouroboros: Notes on Friendship," in *Living the Truth in Love*, ed. Janet E. Smith and Father Paul Check (San Francisco, CA: Ignatius, 2015), 154.

>>———————→ **QUESTION** ←———————《

How do I stay sexually pure on a date?

Dating can be a helpful way to get to know someone, learn more about yourself, and find a potential spouse. But it can also be an opportunity for making decisions you later regret. Here are some helpful steps for dating success. For starters, only date someone who shares your moral and spiritual convictions. Be sure to share your convictions with your date and let them know your boundaries and expectations for dating. Second, don't plan open-ended dates that involve alone time together. Rather, plan dates in public places. Finally, set clear boundaries for physical contact; this will free you up to focus on the relationship.

CHAPTER 6

Understanding Love

What is love?

Endless songs, movies, and poems are about "true love." But can you define it? If not, how would you really know if you are loving someone? And how would you know if you can really believe someone who says, "I love you"?

As a teenager, my father shared a definition of love with me that has helped tremendously throughout my life. If you take the time to understand it, and commit it to heart, it can be a *game-changer* for your life and relationships as well. It comes from the teachings of Paul in Ephesians 5:25–29:

> Husbands, love your wives, as Christ loved the church and gave himself up for her, that he might sanctify her, having cleansed her by the washing of water with the word, so that he might present the church to himself in splendor, without spot or wrinkle or any such thing, that she might be holy and without blemish. In the same way husbands should love their wives as their own bodies. He

who loves his wife loves himself. For no one ever
hated his own flesh, but nourishes and cherishes
it, just as Christ does the church.

In other words, if we want to understand the nature of biblical
love, we need to consider Paul's call for husbands to love their wives
"as Christ loved the church." How did Christ love the church? He
sacrificed his life for her (v. 25). In other words, to understand the
nature of biblical love, we must first look to Christ and what He
did for us on the cross. *Then* we can see how this plays out for us in
Paul's call for husbands to love their wives in the same way as Christ
loved the church.

What does this look like? Paul instructs husbands to love their
wives as they care for their own bodies, which involves *nurturing*
and *cherishing* it. Thus, if we understand what it means to nurture
and cherish our bodies, we have a biblical definition of how a man
is supposed to love his wife.

To *nourish* means to provide for and bring to maturity. It means
to care for someone in their entirety—relationally, physically, spiritually, and socially. Another word for nourish might be "provide."
Love requires that we provide for the best of another person—just
as we naturally provide for our own bodies—in order to bring them
to maturity.

To understand the meaning of *cherish,* imagine a nest of new-
born eaglets high on a mountain crag, exposed to the sky. An angry
thunderstorm is rolling in. The mother eagle swoops down to the
nest and spreads her wings over the eaglets to protect them from
the pounding rain and swirling wind. Simply put, to cherish means
to protect.

Put these two words together and we have the simple definition of love my father shared with me: *to protect and provide.* A husband's love for his wife, which is rooted in the sacrificial love of Christ, aims to protect her from harm and to provide for her good.

This call to protect and provide in marriage is rooted in a broader definition of love: we could say that love is a commitment to the best of another, even if the other does not recognize or accept the reality of the good. This is how husbands are called to love wives, wives are called to love husbands, parents are called to love children, pastors are called to love their congregations, and friends are called to love other friends.

And this is how God loves us. God is committed to our good—*whether or not we recognize that it's our good He's after.* We saw earlier how living the sexual ethic of Jesus would transform societies for the better. But now we see that it is also good for *individuals.* God's commands about sex are meant to protect us from harm and provide for our good.

Consider how following God's loving commands to reserve sex for the marital union of a man and woman both protect and provide for us:

Protection from	Provision for
guilt	freedom
sexual abuse and assault	optimum atmosphere for child-raising
sexually transmitted infections	peace of mind
sexual insecurity	trust
emotional distress	true intimacy

God gives us commands about sex *not* to steal our fun, but to protect and provide for us. God desires to protect us from physical, emotional, and spiritual harm and to provide us with genuine freedom in our relationships.

God gives us commands about sex *not* to steal our fun, but to protect and provide for us.

Nevertheless, the point is not that all sex in marriage is fun. For many couples, it can take years to become comfortable with one another and to develop a pleasurable sex-life. Even then, sometimes sex disappoints.

And the point is not that all sex outside of God's intent is void of being fun. It's not. Interestingly, the Prodigal Son squandered his father's inheritance on wild living without any recognition he was doing wrong until finally "he came to himself" (Luke 15:17). He apparently had fun living in sin for some time. Given the power of sin, it is easy for us to be confused about what is right and what is wrong. Our hearts don't always align with God's standards, and fun is not a good indication of whether we're living obediently or disobediently.

This is what makes our task so difficult today. How do we love people who may not even realize what they are doing is wrong? What does it look like to love people who reject the biblical understanding of love and embrace a cultural understanding? How do we love people who think Christians are bigots?

Let's bring back our definition of love. Remember, love is not a feeling, but a commitment to the best of another, *even if the other does not recognize or accept the reality of the good*. In other words, love does not necessarily imply the person recognizes that we are truly acting in a way that protects and provides for them. In fact, many may even confuse loving actions for hateful ones. After all, people jeered at Jesus on the cross. Love is being committed to the objective good of another regardless of how they feel.

As the designer and creator of sex, God knows how it is to be used for the best for all of us. He knows what is best for you, what is best for me, and what is best for our neighbors. A girl may feel like sleeping with her boyfriend, but it is not best for her to do so. A boy might enjoy looking at porn, but it is not truly good for him. A young person may feel like acting on their same-sex attraction, but despite what our culture proclaims, doing so is not for his or her own good.

Does this mean we are to be the morality police, criticizing others who do not follow the biblical sexual ethic? No, that is not my point. But we must begin by recognizing that love involves a commitment to the good of another, to protect and provide for that person, even if they don't accept it. This gives us courage to speak truth, even when it is unpopular.

We don't speak truth to sound smart, win an argument, or silence people. Rather, we speak truth because *truth is what brings freedom* (John 8:32). And when we speak truth, we are called to do so in love, as Jesus did.

One of my favorite public presentations is what I call "The Atheist Encounter." I put on glasses to role-play an atheist and then respond to audience questions as an atheist might. After about thirty minutes of role-play, I step out of the character to debrief the experience. I always start by asking, "How did you treat the atheist?" Inevitably, the looks on people's faces reveal their realization that they could have been more charitable. The most common words people use to describe how the audience treated the atheist are "disrespectful," "defensive," and "hostile."

After the presentation, one of the most important points I leave audiences with is the task of balancing both grace and truth. *We must speak truth and we must speak it in love* (Eph. 4:15). We can get it wrong on both sides of this equation. We err by speaking truth without grace-filled kindness and genuine concern for others. And we can also get it wrong by watering down truth so as not to offend.

Granted, finding the balance between grace and truth is not always easy. Your generation faces difficult ethical questions today unknown to previous generations: Should you attend a same-sex wedding? Should you use the "proper gender pronoun" for someone who is transgender? And so on. Scripture does not give us simple answers, but Jesus invites us to follow His lead by responding with both grace and truth. Jesus invites us to truly love people, whether they realize it or not.

We must speak truth and we must speak it in love.

For instance, Jesus was criticized for dining with "sinners and tax collectors." Since they were "sinners," Jesus knew they would be more open to His message than self-righteous religious leaders. Thus, rather than requiring them to change their moral behavior *first*, He built loving relationships with them, knowing that they could only experience spiritual transformation after they experienced His grace *firsthand* (Mark 2:13–15).

Jesus showed the same balance of grace and truth in His interaction with the Samaritan woman at the well (John 4). Even though she was both a woman *and* a Samaritan, Jesus reached out to her in relationship. He loved her enough to speak truth, and He did so with kindness.

This balance act of grace and truth is what Jesus invites us to as well. I hope you will join me on this journey. If so, we need to learn how to love people with both our bodies *and* our souls. Let's explore what this means in the next chapter.

>>━━━━━━━→ **QUESTION** ←━━━━━━━<<

How do I know if someone loves me?

Consider a few ways you know someone *does not* love you: if the person pressures you sexually *in any fashion*, treats you rudely, is not interested in you as a whole person, and treats your family or friends with disrespect. Then how do you know if someone *does* love you? Since love involves seeking the best for another, a person who loves you will be interested in protecting and providing for you physically, relationally, and spiritually. While people are not perfect, consider reading 1 Corinthians 13:4–8 and asking whether or not the person aims to treat you accordingly.

CHAPTER 7

Honoring God with Your Body and Soul

A friend of mine has sex with a lot of women. I asked him if the act of sex means anything to him or the girls he's sleeping with, and he nonchalantly said, "No, it's just for fun." In fact, he bragged about the number of women he was pursuing. No matter what I said, he refused to concede that sex had any meaning beyond the physical act itself.

The next time we talked I decided to broach the subject another way. I asked him if he believes a pat on the back means anything. He said it communicates support. Then I asked him if a kiss on the cheek has any meaning, and he said it shows care and affection. Finally, I asked him whether a slap on the face has intrinsic meaning, and he said it's an insult. He agreed these physical acts have *transcultural* meaning—even when they're expressed without any words.

For whatever reason, my next question caught him off guard: "If a kiss on the cheek, slap on the face, and pat on the back have intrinsic meaning, how can the act of sex—which involves the

deepest physical intimacy between two people—not mean anything beyond itself?" He simply stared at me, and then chuckled,
realizing I had a point.

One of the lies of our culture is that we can separate the physical part of being human (the body) from the non-physical part (the
soul). The world says the body carries no inherent meaning and can
be manipulated to whatever we want or think. But life doesn't work
this way. We all know that bodily actions carry *intrinsic* meaning.
We can tell the truth with our bodies, and we can lie with them.

Suppose a used-car salesman sells you a car while withhold-
ing a problem with the transmission, and then shakes your hand.
Did he lie with his body? Of course.[1] Imagine smiling and hugging
someone you deeply dislike. Are you communicating something
you don't really feel? What about a wink at someone you are not
attracted to? Is that a lie? It certainly *can* be.

So, if bodily actions communicate *something*, then what about
sex? If small physical expressions like shaking someone's hand or
winking can be used the wrong way and end up hurting or mis-
leading people, then certainly having sex can communicate all sorts
of wrong things, and hurt a lot of people, when it's used out of its
intended design. It can't really be "just for fun," as my friend suggested. I think we all know better than that.

In the 2001 psychological thriller *Vanilla Sky*, Tom Cruise
plays the role of a rich business owner who falls in love with a girl
he meets at a party. When his current lover finds out they slept
together, she begins stalking him. In one of the more memorable

---

[1] I owe this example to Christopher West, *Theology of the Body* (North
Palm Beach, FL: Wellspring, 2018), 158.

lines from the film, she says, "Don't you know that when you sleep with someone, your body makes a promise whether you do or not." She's right, our bodies communicate. This is true for a kiss on the cheek, a slap on the face, a pat on the back, and *especially* for sex. Sex communicates something profound about trust, vulnerability, and commitment.

Jesus understood the power of human touch. He understood how to use the body to love people. When Jesus healed a paralytic, He simply commanded him, "I say to you, rise, pick up your bed, and go home" (Mark 2:11). Immediately he was healed. That's all he needed, because the paralytic was brought to Jesus by four friends who cared for him.

But when Jesus healed a leper, He *touched* him. Why?

As a leper, the man was considered an outcast from society. According to Jewish law, he had to shout "unclean" and cover his face whenever anyone was near. Thus, he had probably not touched anyone for years. Jesus could have healed him through words alone, as He did the paralytic, but Jesus knew what the affection-starved leper needed most—*touch*. And He touched him in the most appropriate, life-giving way.

We communicate with our bodies and our words because *God has made us both body and soul.* God formed the man "of dust from the ground," breathed into him "the breath of life," and then he became a "living creature" (Gen. 2:7). Hence, a human being has both a physical dimension (body) and a spiritual dimension (soul). We are bodily beings animated by a soul.

It is therefore a mistake to downplay the value of either the body or the soul. One of the first heresies in the early church, Gnosticism, viewed the body and all material things as inherently evil. Gnostics believed that salvation occurs when the soul escapes the "prison house" of the body.

But this is profoundly unbiblical! Genesis 1 tells us that creation—including the human body—is good. Jesus took on *human flesh* to identity with us (Heb. 4:15), show us how to love (John 15:13), and ultimately redeem us (John 3:16).

This is why Scripture calls us to love God and others with our bodies *and* our souls. One way we love God with our souls is learning to think Christianly. Paul said to "not be conformed to this world, but be transformed by the renewal of your mind" (Rom. 12:2). In other words, we are transformed in part by learning to see the world through a biblical perspective. This is one of the main goals of this book—to help you think Christianly about sex, love, and relationships.

Yet we are also called to responsibly steward our bodies. After calling the Corinthian church to avoid sexual immorality, Paul writes, "Do you not know that your body is a temple of the Holy Spirit within you, whom you have from God? You are not your own, for you were bought with a price. So glorify God in your body" (1 Cor. 6:19–20).

Again, Paul writes, "Do not present your members to sin as instruments for unrighteousness, but present yourselves to God as those who have been brought from death to life, and your members to God as instruments for righteousness" (Rom. 6:13). In other words, as believers, we have died to sin and been born as new creations in Christ. Our "old selves" were crucified with Christ, and we have been set free, by grace, to honor God with our bodies.

Interestingly, the motivation to avoid sexual immorality is not primarily because it benefits *you* and *me*. Paul does not tell the

Corinthian church, "Avoid sexual immorality because God's plan is the road to the best sex." As we saw earlier, God's commands *are* for our good. We flourish when we live as God has designed us to live, and there is a strong correlation between following God's plan and experiencing satisfying sex in marriage. But this is not the *motivation* for being sexually pure. Rather, the motivation should be to honor God with our bodies. The question should be: How do we best use our bodies to love God and love other people?

In the United States, abstinence campaigns have often fixated on motivating students to be pure through an *inward focus* on the personal benefits of abstinence (e.g., no disease, better marriage, clear conscience, etc.). Yet in some African-based purity campaigns, the emphasis is more *outward focused* on pleasing God and loving others.[2] Some young people in Africa who aim to keep themselves sexually pure see their bodies as "God's temple" and as a "new creation." Since their bodies are not their own, they aim to engage in a lifestyle that honors God with their bodies. Scripturally speaking, these African young men and young women are on to something important.

If we are called to honor God with our bodies, then for example, shouldn't this influence how we dress? Out of respect for our brothers and sisters in Christ, who aim to love God in both thought and deed, shouldn't we dress with modesty? This is true for both males and females.[3]

---

[2] See Christine J. Gardner, *Making Chastity Sexy: The Rhetoric of Evangelical Abstinence Campaigns* (Berkeley, CA: University of California Press, 2011), 154–57.

[3] Sadly, some people have blamed women in particular, who were victimized by men, because of how they were dressed when sexual harassment occurred. That is emphatically *not* my point. Men are accountable for how they treat women regardless of how they dress. Period.

We are all responsible for our own lustful thoughts. But does this mean we have no responsibility to one another about how we present our bodies? Is it morally neutral to dress in an outfit that invites a lustful gaze? The virtue of modesty invites us to consider that how we dress contributes to broader cultural understanding of morality. Specifically, how can we dress in a way that brings honor to God and helps create a loving environment for others? And this is also true for what we post on social media. Do we post things that honor God with our bodies, or things that potentially cause others to stumble?

You may have noticed that I am not offering a lot of simple answers in this book. My goal is not to give you a list of dos and don'ts. Rather, I am trying to ask the right questions, and frame them from a biblical perspective, so you can work them out in relationships with your Christian friends, family, and church. This book will only have value insofar as you discuss these ideas with key people in your life.

Here's the bottom line: sex means something. Physical touch means something. Humans are body *and* soul. We are thus confronted with a pressing question at the end of this chapter: How do we honor God and love other people with our bodies *and* our souls?

>»——————→ **QUESTION** ←——————«<
Is sex with a robot wrong?

It breaks my heart that this is a relevant question today. While sex with a robot avoids receiving or spreading STIs, there are (at least) three issues to consider. First, such sexual activity would involve sinful lust, which Jesus condemns as immoral (Matt. 5:27–29). Second, it would condition the person to have sex without the presence of another human being. Sex is meant to be experienced between two *people* together in the relationship of marriage. Third, it can shape someone's sexual desires toward a fictionalized robot and away from a real person, potentially bringing dysfunction and addiction into an existing or future relationship.

CHAPTER 8

Distorting God's Plan for Sex

Recently I asked a group of students, "What can people create that lasts the longest?" They paused, reflected, and they gave a few different answers including archaeological remains such as the Egyptian pyramids and Machu Pichu.

Then I followed up with another question: "Can humans create anything that lasts forever?" They reflected again for a brief period, but all agreed that the answer is *no*. After all, they said, everything eventually falls apart. Even though I pressed them for an answer, they concluded that humans are incapable of creating anything that lasts forever.

I simply replied, "I think you are missing something. With God's power, humans can make something that lasts forever— other human beings."

I went on to explain to them, as we saw in the last chapter, that God made humans as *both* body and soul (Matt. 10:28). Physical things in this world do fade away, including our present bodies, but each person has a soul that will never cease to exist, which will be joined to a new body in the resurrection. In fact, after a trillion, trillion, trillion years from now, you will have just as much time left in eternity as you do today. Mind-boggling.

This is why, as my friend Jeremy Pettitt observed, "Sex is the most powerful creative act in the universe. When a man and a woman come together in a sexual relationship, the possibility of creating an eternal soul/spirit arises. At the moment of conception, a new immortal soul/spirit has entered into eternity."[1] Pause, and let this point sink in. Seriously, re-read the last few sentences and make sure you don't miss that. *God has created human beings with the capacity to create something that lasts forever—other human beings.*

This helps explain why C. S. Lewis said there are no ordinary people: "You have never talked to a mere mortal. Nations, cultures, arts, civilization—these are mortal, and their life is to ours as the life of a gnat. But it is immortals whom we joke with, work with, marry, snub, and exploit—immortal horrors or everlasting splendors."[2] The immortal nature of human beings is one reason sex is so sacred and powerful. In sexual union, two people engage in an activity that has the potential of creating another immortal being.

"You have never met a mere mortal."
—C. S. Lewis

---

[1] Jeremy Pettitt, "The Only Thing Humans Create That Lasts Forever," http://jeremypettitt.net/the-only-thing-humans-create-that-lasts-forever (February 11, 2019).
[2] C. S. Lewis, *The Weight of Glory* (HarperOne, 2001), 45–46.

And this is also why Satan is so intent on twisting God's good design for sex. Sex brings new life into the world, yet Satan is a murderer (John 8:44). Children are a blessing that bring hope for the future, yet Satan wants people to be filled with despair. Satan is opposed to God at every turn, and thus has focused so much of his efforts at undermining the goodness, truth, and beauty of sex.

To understand Satan's schemes *today*, we must go back to the Genesis creation story and see what it reveals about his character.

In Genesis 1, we repeatedly learn that creation is good. Water and land are good. Plants are good. Light is good. Animals are good. God makes human beings and commands them to populate the earth (v. 28), and so we can also reasonably conclude that *sex is good*.

God has made a good world so people can populate it and live in loving relationships with Him and with other people.

In Genesis 3, however, Satan shows up, and begins to undermine God's plans for the world. He deceives Adam and Eve and tempts them into disobedience. As a result, sin enters the world and brings incalculable suffering and calamity with it. Three elements of Satan's strategy emerge from this story.

First, *Satan corrupts*. He takes that which God has made good and corrupts it. As the father of lies (John 8:44), Satan corrupts goodness and truth. He corrupts the good purposes of food (nourishment, pleasure) by tempting people to either eat too much (gluttony) or eat too little (anorexia). He corrupts the good purpose of work by tempting people to either ignore it (laziness) or find their identity in it (workaholism).

Satan takes the same corrupting approach to sex, love, and relationships. He corrupts biblical marriage by encouraging divorce.

He corrupts natural human desires by disseminating pornography. He corrupts God's design for humans as gendered beings by undermining the objective reality of male and female. Satan is a corrupter of good.

Second, *Satan deceives*. He is both subtle and cunning in his deception. He did not directly tell Adam and Eve that God is not good. Rather, he asked them questions to *subtly* undermine their confidence in God's character.

Satan appeared as a snake in the garden, but this was before the curse, so they didn't suspect anything unusual. Today, however, Satan masquerades himself as an angel of light (2 Cor. 11:14). He doesn't wear a red suit and carry a pitchfork.

This is why I have little concern my kids will become Satanists! But I am concerned that they are *subtly* being influenced with unbiblical ideas in our culture seeping through music, movies, social media, friends, and a host of other mediums. Why? Because Satan is a subtle deceiver.

Satan is not only subtle; he is also a cunning deceiver. He talked Adam and Eve into doing the wrong thing and convinced them they were doing what was right. Imagine that! Satan is so cunning he can convince people to make wrong choices *and* believe that their wrong choices are actually the right ones. This is why we must not gauge God's Word by our feelings, but rather gauge our feelings by God's Word.

Third, *Satan twists*. The first question Satan asks Adam and Eve is about the words God spoke. "Did God *actually* say, 'You shall not eat of any tree in the garden'?" (Gen. 3:1, emphasis mine). Satan's strategy is to lie, deceive, and *twist* God's words. Sadly, Adam and Eve bought the twisted interpretation of God's Word and ate the fruit. Yet in contrast, when He was tempted, Jesus quoted Scripture—God's Word—back to Satan. Jesus knew Satan twists the words of God, but that true freedom comes from aligning our lives with the truth of Scripture.

Satan still operates today with the same strategy of corrupting God's good design, deceiving people about His character, and twisting His Word. Again, remember, he does this *subtly*. For instance, as we saw at the opening of this chapter, sex matters deeply because it has the potential of creating an eternal being. Sex *is* a big deal. But Satan twists this reality through a variety of cultural mediums, presenting sex as the *biggest* deal. Songs. Memes. Television. Social media. Movies. Advertising. And so on. The "sexual revolution"[3] has tried to convince us that sex is *the* route to happiness. Sex is undoubtedly good, and a wonderful gift from God, but it is not the be-all and end-all of human existence.

On the flip side, Satan has also convinced some believers that sex outside marriage is the worst sin (and thus, practically unforgivable). Sadly, many Christians have adopted a twisted view of God's Word that renders sexual sinners "used goods" incapable of experiencing God's best. But this is also a lie!

Before they were Christians, some Corinthian believers engaged in a range of sexually immoral behavior, such as adultery and homosexual behavior, but Paul still describes them as "washed,"

---

[3] The sexual revolution was a social movement that challenged traditional ideas about sex, love, and marriage. Although seeds were planted much earlier, it is typically dated to the 1960s–1980s. Essentially, supporters used politics, movies, books, and other means to transform culture to be more accepting of sexual behavior outside of heterosexual, marital relationships.

"sanctified," and "justified in the name of the Lord Jesus Christ" (1 Cor. 6:9–11). Sexual sin is serious, and it brings undesirable consequences, but it is not the worst sin. And it is certainly not unforgivable, as we will see in the next chapter.

If reading this book so far has brought up some pain from your own sexual failures, either big or small, please know that *God forgives you when you ask him.* First John 1:9 says, "If we confess our sins, he is faithful and just to forgive us our sins and to cleanse us from all unrighteousness." Even the apostle Paul, who considered himself "the worst of sinners," said that God came into the world through Jesus to save sinners (1 Tim. 1:15–16). That includes *you* and *me.*

God will forgive you for your failings and shortcomings.

If you ask Him, God will forgive you for your failings and shortcomings. If you are willing to confess your sins and ask God to forgive you, *today* you can begin to experience true freedom in Christ. The Christian story, as we will see, is about the relentless pursuit of a loving heavenly Father who wants to see each of us transformed through the power of His grace.

Because experiencing God's grace and forgiveness is so important, we are going to explore it in more depth next chapter.

>>>———————→ **QUESTION** ←———————《
Where should I search for information about sex?

Don't trust Planned Parenthood. While much of their information is not wrong, Planned Parenthood promotes a secular understanding of sex and relationships that undermines the biblical view. Since Planned Parenthood relies upon funding they receive from abortions, they have a built-in incentive to *encourage* sexual activity among young people. Rather, get information from organizations such as the Medical Institute for Sexual Health (https://www.medinstitute.org/) and the Center for Disease Control (CDC). Be careful of trusting public school sex curricula. The state of California, for example, promotes a view of "sexual health" deeply at odds with a Christian view of sex.[4] Lastly, be careful with typing anything related to this subject into Google or another search engine; I would recommend starting by accessing one of the resources I mentioned above.

---

[4] See Sean McDowell, "New California Health Standards Lack Diversity, Inclusion, and Openness," https://seanmcdowell.org/blog/new-california -health-standards-lack-diversity-inclusion-and-openness (Feb. 14, 2019). Also, consider listening to: Sean McDowell and Scott Rae, "Discussing the California Sexual Health Standards," *Think Biblically Podcast*: https:// seanmcdowell.org/podcasts/episode/81 (May 28, 2019).

CHAPTER 9

Experiencing God's Forgiveness

On September 6, 2018, police officer Amber Guyger mistakenly entered the wrong apartment and saw a man sitting on the sofa, watching television. Thinking it was her apartment, she drew her weapon and yelled, "Hands!" and then shot the twenty-six-year-old choir director twice, once in the heart. Guyger was sentenced to ten years in prison for the death of Botham Jean.

Roughly a year later at the trial, the teenage brother of Botham Jean captured the attention of the entire nation through his powerful words and actions. "I forgive you," said Brandt Jean, "and I know that if you go to God and ask Him, He will forgive you . . . I love you just like anyone else . . . I personally want the best for you," said the young man.

"I don't even want you to go to jail," Brandt declared. "I want the best for you because I know that's exactly what Botham would want you to do . . . and the best would be: give your life to Christ."

With tears in his eyes, he turned to the judge and asked if he could *please* give her a hug. The judge agreed, and while sobbing,

Guyger fell into the arms of the young man who had just shown her tender grace and forgiveness.

Even though I was sitting in the seat of a plane, I couldn't hold back the tears while watching this courtroom scene unfold. It felt as if time froze because this young man so beautifully captured the grace and forgiveness God shows to each one of us, including *you* and *me*.

Before we enter the next section of this book and explore God's specific design for sex, singleness, and marriage, it is incumbent that we pause to ensure God's love and forgiveness has penetrated our own hearts. Why is this so important? Because there are two hugely important things we will never be able to do until we personally experience God's grace and forgiveness.

First, we will not be able to genuinely love others.

In Matthew 18:21–35, Jesus tells the story of a servant who had been forgiven a massive debt from the king. Rather than enslaving the man and his family, the king mercifully forgave him his debt. Yet shortly thereafter, the same servant went out to another servant who owed him a much smaller debt and had him thrown in prison for not paying it back. When the king learned what the first servant had done, he threw him in prison and scolded him for failing to be as merciful to his fellow servant as the king had been to him.

Jesus told this story because Peter asked Him how often he should forgive a brother who sins against him. Forgive the "small" sins others commit against you, Jesus says, because God has forgiven you a "massive" debt. Thus, when we understand how much grace God has shown us, we can naturally extend grace to others. Brandt Jean was able to extend forgiveness to Amber Guyger because he had personally experienced God's forgiveness in his own life.

Christians are often accused of being harsh, judgmental, homophobic, and bigoted toward others who hold a different sexual ethic. Sometimes these claims are dishonest strategies meant to silence Christians for their views. But sometimes these claims are true.

We as a church have often failed to live as God desires us to live. Porn is an issue in the church. Some people have been treated ungraciously because of their particular sexual struggles. Gossip is prevalent. Pride. Lust. Divorce. And so on. The church is not immune to the sins of the world. And by the way, the church is not a building—*it includes you and me.*

My point is not to beat up on the church (I love the church!). And my point is not to make you feel unnecessarily guilty. The point is that we must first ask ourselves if we have seen our own sin and known our desperate need for forgiveness, and if we have turned to Christ for that forgiveness and found His freeing grace, so we can be agents of grace to others. Recognizing the depth of our own sin will help us be more loving to other people.

Recognizing the depth of our own sin will help us be more loving to other people.

The second thing we won't be able to do until we've personally experienced God's grace and forgiveness is get out of the cycle of guilt and shame that we've all experienced. Until we experience God's grace, we will remain enslaved to sin, unable to break free.

I have had countless conversations with young people overburdened by guilt and shame. So many young people today feel like "used goods" or a "hopeless cause" because of sexual activity, habitually looking at porn, or some other shortcoming in their lives. My response is always the same:

> *God loves you. God is ready to forgive you. God does not look at you as used goods but as His beautiful creation that He yearns to be in relationship with. Scripture promises that if we confess our sins, God is faithful and just to forgive us. Period. Jesus wants you to be free from shame and guilt, which is why He invited those who are heavy laden and weary to come to Him and receive rest. That invitation is to you.*

How can I have such confidence? The answer is because of what Jesus did on the cross.

Crucifixion was the most painful and shameful death imaginable. Victims were stripped naked and publicly humiliated. Even though He was innocent, Jesus did this willingly for you and me.

In contrast, when Adam and Eve sinned in the garden, they hid and covered themselves with fig leaves to hide their shame. God then exchanged their fig leaves with the covering of animal skin, which was the first death in Scripture (Gen. 3:21). But then in the ultimate act of redemption, God exchanged *their* nakedness through His *own* nakedness on the cross.

As weird as this may seem, especially if you haven't thought about it, Jesus was actually naked on the cross. Even though our pictures and statues have Jesus clothed, we know that Romans would strip crucifixion victims so they would be utterly shamed in public.

Jesus not only experienced excruciating physical pain, He also experienced the depth of human shame. If you have ever felt shame from your choices, you can be assured that Jesus understands.

Why would He do this? The answer is simple: He willingly experienced the depth of human sin through public torture, humiliation, and shame so we could experience freedom from our shame. Jesus held nothing back so we could be forgiven.

Whether this has crossed your mind or not, the point is not that we should unclothe Jesus on the cross. This might even raise more problems than it would solve! But we should at least be aware—and reflective—of how far Jesus went to cover our shame. Consider a few personal questions:

> Do you really believe that Jesus took upon Himself all of your sexual failures on the cross? And I mean all of them.

> Do you understand that He was willing to be publicly humiliated to release you from the guilt and shame of your sins? Yes, this includes porn use, abortion, sexual abuse, unjustified divorce, homosexual behavior, and every other sexual sin you can imagine.

> Do you really believe that you have a high priest who can understand the depth of your humiliation and shame (Heb. 2:18; 4:15)?

No matter what you have done, or what has been done to you, if you are trusting Jesus for forgiveness, please know that God forgives you. God is not a harsh king who gets pleasure in judging us, but a loving heavenly Father who yearns for us to be in relationship with Him and other people, and to experience the freedom that comes from forgiveness. God wants you to have a fresh start. And that fresh start can begin today.

»————————→ QUESTION ←————————«
How can I feel forgiven?

You may feel pain, guilt, and shame from sexual sin. The first step to feeling forgiven is to be sure you have confessed your sins to the Lord and cried out for His mercy. Scripture says that we have all sinned (Rom. 3:23), but that God will forgive us if we ask (1 John 1:9). If you have confessed your sins, then He forgives you. *You* are forgiven. Consider meditating on 1 John 2:1 and Psalm 103:12 and confessing to a trusted leader who can pray with you, encourage you, and will help you feel God's forgiveness firsthand.

PART 2

CHAPTER 10

Loving Others with Our Sexuality

Jesus was a sexual human being.

Does this claim strike you as bizarre? Maybe even *heretical*? Before you react, let me explain.

In his excellent book *Mere Sexuality*, Todd Wilson argues that Christians often fail to reflect on how the humanity of Jesus should inform our understanding of sexuality. We focus on Jesus as divine and tend to forget He was also truly human just like us.

Wilson calls this the "Clark Kent is really Superman" view of Jesus. As you might recall, Superman is not really a human being, although he appears to be one. Rather, he was born of an alien race on the planet Krypton. He wears a disguise to pretend that he is human (Clark Kent) even though his true nature is Kryptonian. He can relate to us, but Superman does not really know what it is like to be human.

But unlike Superman, Jesus didn't merely *pretend* to be human. He did not put on a human body and disguise Himself as a man. Scripture teaches that Jesus was human in *every* way—eating, sleeping, being tempted—and yet was without sin (Heb. 2:14–18). Jesus was both God *and* man.

And this means that Jesus, like the rest of us, was a sexual human being. This does *not* mean he was sexually active, but it does mean that Jesus had a sexed body. Wilson explains:

> Through the incarnation, God the Son has a Y chromosome, facial hair, a higher basal metabolism rate—all the physiology, anatomy, and biochemistry that are distinctive to being a male . . . the Word of God took on a particular kind of human flesh—the kind that goes through puberty, grows armpit hair, has a ring finger longer than his index finger, a deeper voice than most women, and a penis.[1]

I want to emphasize (as does Wilson) that this does not mean that boys are better than girls. Sorry guys, but that is *not* the point! Rather, the point is that when God chose to fully reveal Himself to us, He entered into the human race with a sexed human body, affirming the goodness of human sexuality.

Jesus not only came as a man, but He also came into human nature *through* the womb of a woman. Again, Wilson explains:

> By embracing human nature, God the Son embraced the Virgin's womb. The Second Person of the Trinity swam in amniotic fluid, fed from an umbilical cord, traveled a vaginal canal, and fed at

---

[1] Todd Wilson, *Mere Sexuality: Rediscovering the Christian Vision of Sexuality* (Grand Rapids, MI: Zondervan, 2017), 45.

> his mother's breast . . . Through the incarnation,
> God the Son embraced male and female sexuality
> to the core. He didn't sidestep human sexuality;
> rather, he embraced it fully.[2]

This is vitally important for three reasons. First, human sexuality is good. God made human beings as male *and* female, and then announced that His creation was "very good" (Gen. 1:31). Jesus took on male human flesh, entering through the womb of a woman, thus confirming the goodness of male and female sexuality.

Throughout church history, some have suggested that sexual differences and procreation resulted from the fall. Yet Genesis 1:27–28 makes it clear God created humans as male and female and commanded them to multiply and fill the earth *before* the entrance of sin. He made human beings as male and female *from the beginning*. God created two sexes and considers that "good."

Second, in taking on human flesh as a sexed being, Jesus showed that male sexuality and female sexuality depend upon one another. As Paul says, "Nevertheless, in the Lord woman is not independent of man nor man of woman; for as woman was made from man, so man is now born of woman" (1 Cor. 11:11–12). Men and women depend upon each other for their existence. In taking on male flesh, yet being born *through* a woman, Jesus affirmed the interdependence and importance of male *and* female sexuality.

Third, in becoming a human being, Jesus came to understand our struggles and can help us through them. Hebrews 4:15 says, "For we do not have a high priest who is unable to sympathize with our weaknesses, but one who in every respect has been tempted as

---

[2] Ibid., 46.

we are, yet without sin." As a human being, Jesus experienced temptation, including sexual temptation. And yet He endured without sinning. Thus, God understands the depths of our temptations and promises to sustain us through them if we humbly ask Him and rely upon His grace (1 Cor. 10:13).

In becoming a human being, Jesus came to understand our struggles and can help us through them.

Yet this is only the beginning. Not only was Jesus born as a male, as we have seen, but He rose with the *same* male body, although it was transformed into a resurrection body (see 1 Cor. 15:20–49). Jesus continued to be both human and male after His resurrection (see Luke 24:39). Thus, while marriage and sexual intercourse will no longer exist in heaven (Matt. 22:30), human beings will continue as male or female forever, *as Jesus does.* Again, Wilson explains,

> When the Son chose a Y chromosome and embraced human flesh, he did so forever—never to take it off or hang it up like an old worn-out coat. Our humanity, including our sexual difference, has become an intrinsic part of who God the Son is—and who God the Son will be forever.[3]

Jesus was not sexually active, but He did experience the world as a *sexed* human being. His sexuality shaped how He related to His

---

[3] Ibid., 48.

mom, His apostles, and His female followers. This is important because it demonstrates that sexuality goes much deeper than simply "having sex."

We tend to reduce sex to the physical act of sexual intercourse, but our sexuality encompasses much more. Sexuality refers to how we understand and experience the world as males and females. We can express our sexuality through sexual activity, including the way we touch others and speak to them. But we also express our sexuality through ordinary, non-sexual actions such as how we dress, talk, and comb our hair. Sexuality pervades all of our relationships including siblings, parents, teachers, and friends.

Think about it: If you are a girl, don't you relate to your mother differently than your father? If you are a boy, don't you relate to a brother differently than a sister? Of course. My kids relate to me differently than they do my wife. It is inescapable: *Our existence as males and females influences all of our relationships.* Although our culture seeks to deny and ignore differences between boys and girls, it is only when we under-

Our existence as males and females influences all of our relationships.

stand sex differences that we can love people for who they truly are.

Reducing sexuality to sex misses a deeper truth about what it means to be human. Whether we are married or single, sexually active or celibate, all of us are designed by God as sexual beings. We experience the world through our sexuality. As Christopher West has observed, "Sex is not first what people *do*. It is who people *are* as male or female."[4]

Now that we understand the difference between *sexuality* and *sexual activity*, it is important to explore the purpose of sex, single-ness, and marriage. That is what we will do in the next few chapters.

»——————→ QUESTION ←——————«
Is cybersex wrong?

Also known as virtual sex, cybersex is when two or more people engage in sexual arousal through digital technology such as a video chat, email, phone, texting, social media, or virtual reality. Since virtual sex involves sexual activity, it is wrong to practice it outside the context of marriage. Further, since sending or receiving sexual images of a minor is considered child pornography, it is illegal for people under eighteen to practice certain kinds of virtual sex. Married couples should also be wise and discerning about potentially engaging in virtual sex together.

---

[4] Christopher West, *Theology of the Body: Rediscovering the Meaning of Life, Love, Sex, and Gender* (North Palm Beach, FL: Wellspring, 2018), 98.

CHAPTER 11

The Purpose of Sex

A number of years ago, my mom got a new computer and decided to set up her own email account. One of the first instructions on the screen said, "Close all the windows." Not understanding the intent of the message, my mom got up from her chair and closed all the windows in the *house*.

No, I am not joking.

Since she is a Baby Boomer, digital technology does not come as naturally to my mom as it does to my teenage son (although she has come a long way since this incident!). Thus, we can forgive her failure to properly understand what the message on the computer screen was *for*.

In chapter 4, we explored the difference between "freedom from" and "freedom for." Freedom *from* is having the ability to make choices without constraint; freedom *for* is about using something according to its purpose. The person who understands the purpose of a computer, for instance, and uses it properly, is the freest.

This also applies to sex. I am not intending to trivialize the importance of sex by comparing it to a computer. I simply want to emphasize that the only way to know how we should act sexually toward others is to first answer the question, "What is sex *for*?"

Some atheists hold that sex is merely the fulfillment of a natural animal instinct that we have inherited from our evolutionary ancestors. The purpose of sex, in this view, is merely to pass on one's genes to the next generation to foster the "survival of the species." But while the sex drive is necessary for survival, the meaning of sex goes much deeper than animal instinct.

According to God—the creator of sex—there are three primary purposes for sex.

Procreation

It should come as no surprise that sex is about making babies. Genesis 1:28 makes this clear. After creating humans as male and female, God blessed them and said, "Be fruitful and multiply and fill the earth and subdue it."

This is both a blessing from God *and* a command. In all my years teaching, speaking, and counseling students, I have never heard one complain about *this* command!

It is worth noting that sex between a man and a woman is a procreative act *even if a child does not result*. Some opposite-sex couples are infertile, and thus unable to have kids. Yet, when they are sexually active, their bodies nonetheless unite in a way that is *oriented* toward procreation, even if the woman does not become pregnant. But this is not true for same-sex couples. They cannot engage in procreative sex with one another because their bodies are not mutually oriented toward procreation by design.

Simply put, there is a difference between an action that fails to produce its intended outcome (infertile opposite-sex sexual activity) and an action that cannot produce an intended outcome by its very nature (same-sex sexual activity).

Whether a child results or not, sex between a man and woman is oriented toward the procreation of new life.

Unity

One of the most powerful aspects of sex is its ability to bond people together. Genesis 2:24 says, "Therefore a man shall leave his father and his mother and hold fast to his wife, and they shall become one flesh." When a couple has sex, something changes in their relationship. They have entered into a deeper unity that is not only spiritual, but also emotional, relational, and even biochemical (which is one reason it is especially difficult for teenagers to break up after they have been sexually active).

Scientific research has recently confirmed that this bonding takes place on a neurochemical level. A key neurochemical important to healthy sex and bonding is oxytocin. The release of oxytocin generates bonding and trust with another person.

While oxytocin occurs in both genders, it is most prominent in women. A woman's body is flooded with oxytocin during labor and breast-feeding. The presence of oxytocin produces a chemical impact in the mother's brain that a woman experiences as the "motherly bond" with her child. A woman's body is also flooded with oxytocin during intimate physical touch and sexual activity, causing her to desire touch again and again with the man to whom she has bonded, generating an even stronger connection.

Oxytocin helps build the trust that is essential for a lasting, healthy relationship.

This is partly why sexual activity with multiple partners raises the risk of negative emotional consequences for young women in particular. Dr. Joe McIlhaney and Dr. Freda McKissic Bush conclude: "The adolescent girl who enters into a close physical relationship may, therefore, find herself, because of the normal effect of her brain hormones and the brain molding that results, desiring more physical contact and trusting a male who may be using manipulative pledges of love and care only to get her to have sex with him."[1]

God has designed sex to help bond a man and his wife together *for life*.

But what about pleasure? God certainly designed sex to be pleasurable. Think about it: God could have made sexual activity boring, like taking out the trash, but instead He made it one of the most exhilarating human experiences. God made sexual activity pleasurable as a gift to human beings.

God has designed sex to help bond a man and his wife together *for life*.

While sex is pleasurable, there are many other things in life that also give us pleasure, such as exercise, reading, and eating. The *purpose* of eating, for instance, is to absorb nutrients for survival. If the purpose of eating were pleasure, then it would seem that someone could eat anything

---

[1] Joe S. McIlhaney and Freda McKissic Bush, *Hooked: The Brain Science on How Casual Sex Affects Human Development* (Chicago, IL: Northfield, 2019), 37.

that felt good, without regard for how it benefitted the body. But that is a recipe for disaster!

To determine whether it is good to exercise a particular pleasure or not, we have to look beyond the experience of pleasure to the nature of the act itself. Many things feel good that are not right (ever felt a thrill from breaking the rules?). Sexual activity outside of marriage can—and often *does*—feel good. But that does not make it right. Nor does it make it good.

When experienced according to God's design, sex is undeniably pleasurable. But pleasure is not the purpose of sex; rather, it provides the *motivation* for engaging in it.

Foreshadowing Heaven

The Bible begins with a wedding between Adam and Eve (Gen. 2). The apostle Paul tells us that marriage has existed since creation to point us to the mysterious union between Christ and the church (see Eph. 5:30–31). Human history even culminates with the "marriage of the Lamb," which is the heavenly wedding of Christ, who is the groom, and the church, who is the bride (Rev. 19:7). Why is this so important?

Christopher West notes, "The union of the sexes—as beautiful and wonderful as it is in the divine plan—is only a faint glimmer, a pale picture within time of the eternal union with God."[2] As we saw earlier in this chapter, the "one-flesh" union of a man and woman is a bond that entails an emotional, relational, spiritual, *and*

---

[2] Christopher West, *Theology of the Body: Rediscovering the Meaning of Life, Love, Sex, and Gender* (North Palm Beach, FL: Wellspring, 2018), 99.

physical element. When people focus merely on the physical element, they miss the deeper unity—the intimate connection—that occurs between two people in the act of sex. It is *this* kind of holistic union that foreshadows the kind of *greater* union we will have with God and others in heaven.

The cultural obsession with sex today misses its deeper purpose of foreshadowing our union with God in heaven. From music to movies to social media, sex is everywhere. Since our culture has lost the transcendent meaning of sex, many people today think that sex *itself* is the route to happiness. Thus, rather than worshipping the Creator (of sex), people today worship the created thing (sex). The Bible calls this idolatry (see Rom. 1:18–32).

Have you ever been to the Grand Canyon? If you have, you know it is absolutely a sight to behold—arguably the most gorgeous and breathtaking natural environment in the United States. People staring at the Canyon are in awe of it, and seeing it is worth the hours it might take you to get there.

Back in the day, if you wanted to take a trip to somewhere like the Grand Canyon, you'd have to buy a paper map. From my home in California, it would be about an eight-hour drive, and the map would take me across I-10 and I-40 into Arizona. Now, can you imagine if I bought a map with directions to the Grand Canyon, and then framed the map on my wall and never actually went? How foolish would I be if every morning, as I drank my morning coffee, I stared at that map basking in the glory of a trip to the Grand Canyon, but never intended to actually go?

Believe it or not, *this is exactly how people treat sex.* The gift of sex—like all of God's good gifts—is meant to point us to the Giver. It is merely a foretaste of what awaits us, like a road map or a signpost to some glorious destination. The road map is not the point; the destination is. Don't settle for cheap thrills when there is an everlastingly satisfying God who gives us good things to point us and draw us to Himself!

Here is something our culture desperately misses: *Even the most wonderful sex life cannot satisfy the craving of the human heart for love and connection.* I have been married to my wife for more than two decades. I thank God for my caring, loving, and beautiful bride. Yet she is not my ultimate fulfillment. And I am not hers. We both know that any human relationship—including our own—cannot ultimately fulfill the deepest yearning of our hearts for love and relationship. And the same is true for *you.*

Because of how much I love my wife, I am tempted to be disappointed that there is no marriage or sex in heaven (see Matt. 22:30). My single friends tell me they often fear that, by not getting married or having sex, they are missing out on something good. Given how much our culture worships sex, these feelings are understandable.

Even the most wonderful sex life cannot satisfy the craving of the human heart for love and connection.

But we must remember that the sexual union merely *foreshadows* something far greater yet to come. As wonderful as it is, sex anticipates the deeper fulfillment that all believers will experience with God and others in heaven.

This doesn't mean that heaven involves endless sexual bliss (as some Muslims describe it). It simply means that sexual union on

Earth is a pointer, an anticipation, a foreshadowing of a deeper union we will all experience in heaven.

Can you see why Satan is so intent on twisting the nature of sex? If he can confuse people about sex, he can confuse them about heaven.

In sum, the purpose of sex is three-fold: procreation, unity, and the anticipation of heaven. Understanding these truths and orienting our lives around them sets us free to experience love, sex, and relationships as God designed them to be experienced.

Before we move to discuss the purpose of singleness and marriage, let's consider three of the biggest myths about sex.

≫———————→ **QUESTION** ←———————≪

*How effective are condoms in
preventing pregnancy and STIs?*

Condoms help reduce the chance of pregnancy, but they do not eliminate it. The effectiveness of condoms depends upon factors such as consistent use, lack of damage, the kind of condom, and the frequency of sex. Roughly one in five teens using condoms become pregnant within one year.[3] Condoms can help prevent transmission of some STIs, but herpes, gonorrhea, HPV, and other infections are spread through sexual contact not protected by a condom, such as mutual masturbation, oral sex, and anal sex.

---

[3] McIlhaney and Bush, *Hooked: The Brain Science on How Casual Sex Affects Human Development*, 83.

CHAPTER 12

Myth 1: Sex Is Not a Big Deal

Planned Parenthood recently launched an online chatbot named "Roo" to answer student questions about sex, pregnancy, and other sexual health issues. One of the questions initially trending on the site was, "What's the right age to have sex for the first time?"

The answer Roo offers is, "It's all about picking the right age for you, which might be totally different than the right age for other people. It may seem like everybody you know is having sex, but that's definitely not true. The average age when people have sex for the first time is around seventeen."

When I shared this with a group of high school students, a senior made the perceptive observation that Planned Parenthood *assumes* sex is not a big deal. There is no mention of marriage, commitment, or children. Sex is portrayed entirely as an activity dependent on the relative feelings of the individual. If you feel ready, then go for it.

At the heart of the "sexual revolution" has been the idea that sex is not a big deal. It's simply a recreational activity for consenting adults, like any other. But I think we know better.

Not long ago, I read an interview about two major Hollywood figures who filmed a sex scene together for a PG-13 film. Since the actress had not performed a scene like this before, she shared in the interview that she got drunk beforehand to dull her discomfort. In fact, she felt so vulnerable that she called her mom the night before and asked her to tell her that everything would be okay.

At the heart of the "sexual revolution" has been the idea that sex is not a big deal.

The actor also felt discomfort. In an interview for a popular entertainment channel, he was asked about how he cared for his female co-star during the filming of the sex scene. Quite understandably, he fumbled around for an answer, and then moved on rather quickly.

If sex is not a big deal, as sexual revolutionaries such as Planned Parenthood imply, then why should they feel uncomfortable filming a sex scene in the first place? Why does the interviewer ask him about his comfort level when filming *this* scene, but not his comfort level for different scenes, such as when they walk down the hall together or eat dinner as a couple?

The fact that she got drunk before this scene, and the interviewer felt the need to ask him how he cared for his co-star during *this* scene, shows that everyone knows there's something inherently important, vulnerable, and powerful happening in sexual intimacy, and that no one really believes sex is just another physical activity. We intuitively know sex matters, and that it is not a recreational activity like any other. We all know that sex *is* a big deal.

>>————→ **QUESTION** ←————《
What's the big deal with a hookup?

A hookup is when two people get together for a sexual encounter without expecting anything further in the relationship. What's the big deal? Consider three factors. First, there are often *emotional* consequences. Since sex binds people together, many people feel used and empty after a hookup. The heart is designed to want more in a relationship. Second, there can be *physical* consequences, such as STIs and pregnancy. Third, since a hookup involves using someone for your own pleasure rather than truly loving that person, there are *spiritual* consequences in your life as well. Hookups matter, and we all know it.

CHAPTER 13

Myth 2: Sex Is Merely a Private Act

One of the most popular tourist campaigns in history was driven by the famous tagline, "What happens in Vegas stays in Vegas." The campaign has encouraged millions of people to think they can experience a kind of anonymity and freedom in Las Vegas that they can't achieve in their daily lives.

A few years ago, I was flying home and had a stopover in Las Vegas. As the plane was about to land, the flight attendant said, "Remember, what happens in Vegas . . . shows up on YouTube the next day."

The plane erupted in laughter, partly because of the element of surprise, but also because there is *truth* in the observation. People may want to believe that their actions in Vegas stay private, but in reality, we know this is false.

One of the most common mantras of the sexual revolution is that sex is entirely a private act between consenting adults. As such, there should be no criticism or regulation; what consenting adults do behind closed doors is up to them.

In other words, "What happens in the bedroom stays in the bedroom."

There is certainly *some* truth in this assertion. After all, sex is not meant to be a public act. Like going to the bathroom or taking a shower, sex is meant to be experienced in privacy. Nevertheless, it is impossible to separate the private act of sex from its public consequences. Let's consider three examples.

First, *sexually transmitted infections* (STIs). According to the Centers for Disease Control (CDC) roughly 20 million new sexually transmitted infections occur every year in America, half of them in young people ages fifteen to twenty-four.[1] The U.S government ment spends billions per year on research and treatment for STDs. Quite obviously, this is an expense that everyone pays for— sexually active or not. And there is also a cost for human life. In 2017, there were 94 infant deaths related to syphilis.[2] Sadly, these newborns lost their lives because of what their parents did "behind closed doors."

Sex is a big deal, as we have seen, and thus our sexual experiences shape the development of our character.

---

[1] "Adolescents and Young Adults" (Dec. 7, 2017): https://www.cdc.gov/std/life-stages-populations/adolescents-youngadults.htm (accessed Nov. 4, 2019).

[2] Jacqueline Howard, "Three STDs Reach All-Time Highs in the US, New CDC Report Says," CNN (Oct. 8, 2019): https://www.cnn.com/2019/10/08/health/std-cases-rising-us-study/index.html (accessed Nov. 4, 2019).

Second, *children*. Sex is the natural means by which humans procreate. Since sex has the potential of creating new life, a result that affects the entire community, it cannot be limited to the walls of the bedroom. Sex quite literally affects *everyone*.

Third, *character*. Our sexual experiences deeply shape our character. Sex is a big deal, as we have seen, and thus our sexual experiences shape the development of our character and influence how we treat other people beyond the bedroom. Given how vulnerable people are in sex, it is impossible to separate our private experiences from the development of our public character. And our character shapes everything we do.

Sex may be practiced in private. But for at least these three reasons, it is the concern of the whole community.

What happens in the bedroom does *not* stay in the bedroom.

>>——————→ **QUESTION** ←——————<<

How easy is it to get an STI?

The best way to prevent STIs is to be abstinent, including from oral sex, anal sex, and other sexual touching. If you are sexually active, you have a greater likelihood of acquiring an STI than you may realize. In a given year, fifteen- to twenty-four-year olds make up half of the 20 million new cases of STIs.[3] For the past five years, combined cases of syphilis, gonorrhea, and chlamydia have hit record highs.[4] STIs can be acquired by *one* sexual episode. And they can be spread when there are no symptoms. Most people who have an STI do not know it.

---

[3] US Department of Health and Human Services, "Adolescent Development and STDs," https://www.hhs.gov/ash/oah/adolescent-development/reproductive-health-and-teen-pregnancy/stds/index.html#_ftn1.

[4] David Nield, "The US Just Hit Another High in STD Rates, and You Need to Protect Yourself," *Science Alert* (October 12, 2019), https://www.sciencealert.com/the-us-hits-another-record-high-in-std-rates-as-the-shocking-trend-continues.

CHAPTER 14

Myth 3: Sexual Intercourse Is All That Matters for Purity

Some time ago I had a conversation with a young man who told me he was a virgin. Yet when I pressed the discussion further (in an effort to answer another question he asked me), it was clear he had gone to considerable lengths sexually with a girl, even though they had never had intercourse. Was he *really* a virgin?

Answering this question, of course, depends on what we mean by the term *virgin*. Technically, a virgin is someone who has not had sexual intercourse. But this definition raises further questions: Does oral sex count as sexual intercourse? What about anal sex? What about mutual masturbation? These activities are unmistakably *sexual* in nature, but do they disqualify someone from being a virgin?

To me, the debate over whether or not someone "qualifies" as a virgin seems misguided, and even potentially harmful. Many young people who have wrongly engaged in sexual activity, either before they became Christians or after, have felt second-rate, as if they are "used goods." Some feel they have been permanently stained by their sexual failures because they are no longer virgins.

But this is *not* how the Bible categorizes people! If you are a Christian, and have asked God for forgiveness, then you are "a new creation. The old has passed away; behold, the new has come" (2 Cor. 5:17). To the Christians at Corinth, many of whom had engaged in wrongful sexual activity, Paul said, "You were washed, you were sanctified, you were justified in the name of the Lord Jesus Christ and by the Spirit of our God" (1 Cor. 6:11).

I realize it can be scary to discover you've been acting against God's desire for your life, but you don't have to be afraid of Him. He's your loving Father who is ready with open arms to restore you. Run toward Him, not away from Him. God is eager to forgive and restore you.

This is not to say that various kinds of sexual activity are unimportant. Sadly, this young man adopted the idea that virtually *any* sexual behavior was permissible outside marriage except intercourse. How had he gotten this idea? Clearly not from Scripture.

Genesis 4:1 says that "Adam knew Eve his wife." In Hebrew, the word translated "knew" is *yada*. The word is an idiom for sexual intercourse in the Old Testament, but it carries the connotation of a deeper relational union involving the mind, soul, *and* body. The Jewish understanding is that sex is a holistic activity in which the body cannot be separated from the mind or soul.

This is why Paul instructs believers to avoid sexual immorality with their *bodies* (e.g., 1 Cor. 6:13; Rom. 6:13). Yet he also instructs them to be pure in *mind*: "Brothers, whatever is true, whatever is honorable, whatever is just, whatever is pure, whatever is lovely, whatever is commendable, if there is any excellence, if there is anything worthy of praise, think about these things" (Phil. 4:8).

Let me ask you a few questions: Do you think it's possible to be thinking about "whatever is pure" while engaging in oral sex? Is it possible to be thinking about things that are "worthy of praise" while letting your hands wander all over a girl whose body belongs to God (and not you)? Is it possible to be thinking about "whatever is honorable" while engaging in mutual masturbation? If we are honest with ourselves, I think we know the answers.

Sexual activity with someone you're not married to will always be tinged with guilt and regret because it's a misuse of God's design for sex. Instead, imagine the beauty of sexual activity with a spouse that will be completely pure, that doesn't make you feel guilty, that you can do openly before God because it is celebrated by Him! Don't settle for the cheap imitation of uncommitted sexual activity. God wants better for *you*.

Don't settle for the cheap imitation of uncommitted sexual activity.

God wants each of us to be pure in body, soul, *and* mind. He is not interested in mere technical virginity, but in us loving Him, and other people, with *all* of our selves.

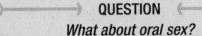

QUESTION
What about oral sex?

Many teenagers choose to engage in oral sex to enjoy the thrills of sex but avoid pregnancy. While you can't get pregnant from giving or receiving oral sex, it *is* sexual activity. That's why they call it oral *sex*. Consequences? Oral sex puts you at risk of acquiring STIs. Girls who give oral sex often feel used by boys and are left with feelings of anger, shame, and guilt. Like other kinds of sexual activity, oral sex bonds you with a partner and can give you feelings of loneliness when the relationship is over.

CHAPTER 15

The Purpose of Singleness

You might be wondering why there is a chapter on singleness in a book on sex, love, and marriage. After all, isn't the goal to get married in the future and "live happily ever after"? We will explore the nature of marriage in an upcoming chapter, so I will refrain from commenting on this fairy-tale view of marriage for the time being.

But for now, consider two reasons why we *must* discuss singleness. First, as we will see below, singleness and marriage are equal ways of serving and honoring God. Neither is better, or more important, than the other. We need both married couples *and* single people in the church. Although it surprises many people in our culture, the apostle Paul described singleness as a gift for the church (1 Cor. 7:8).

Second, everyone is single for at least a season in their life. If you are a teenager right now, and want to get married someday, you will likely be single for many years to come. In fact, if you're a younger teen, you are statistically *halfway* there. That can seem like a long time! Thus, we must honestly wrestle with the question: How can you honor God in your single life *right now*?

Yet even if you get married someday, you will likely be single again. Unfortunately, rarely do spouses die at the same time. And unfortunately, many marriages end in divorce. Given that you are single right now, and likely will be for a significant season in your life, we need to consider what it means for single people to love God and love other people.

Not long ago, I heard a pastor claim that the best way to serve God today is through getting married and having kids. This kind of message is not uncommon in the church today. While loving marriages are undoubtedly a powerful way of representing the relationship between Christ and the church to the world and reaching relationally broken people today, I sat there wondering about my single friends. If marriage is the *best* way to serve God, then are single people necessarily relegated to secondary status? Moreover, since Jesus never got married, did He fail to embrace the most effective means of outreach? Clearly not.

Sadly, in both teaching and practice, the church often idolizes marriage.

The wider culture is also suspicious about singles who remain sexually abstinent. The premise of the movie *The 40-Year-Old Virgin* is that there is something laughable about an adult who has not had sex. It's unthinkable to be a virgin at forty years old! In the film, people are stunned to learn that the main character—played by Steve Carrell—is an adult virgin.

This is why it can be so hard for single people today who want to honor the Lord! They seem at odds with both the marriage emphasis of the church and the sex-obsessed focus of our culture.

And yet Scripture takes us beyond this false dichotomy. The apostle Paul considers both singleness and marriage as equal *gifts* for the church. Both can be beautiful ways of loving God and loving other people.

In 1 Corinthians 7, Paul tells believers at Corinth that he wishes they could all be single like him. "But," he says, "each has his own gift from God, one of one kind and one of another" (v. 7). The two gifts Paul discusses here are singleness and marriage. His point is not that some people have the "gift" of singleness understood as a supernatural ability to remain content without marriage. Rather, Paul emphasizes that both singleness *and* marriage are important gifts to build up the church. Singleness is good. Marriage is good. Both deeply benefit the church.

In his book *Singles at the Crossroads,* Albert Hsu explains, "*If you are single, then you have the gift of singleness. If you are married, you don't.* If you marry, you exchange the gift of singleness for the gift of marriedness. Both are good. Simple as that."[1]

The apostle Paul considers both singleness and marriage as equal *gifts* for the church. Both can be beautiful ways of loving God and loving other people.

---

[1] Albert Hsu, *Singles at the Crossroads* (Downers Grove, IL: InterVarsity Press, 1997), 58.

Marriage and singleness are both gifts for the church, and they both require a unique kind of sacrifice. As a husband and father, I have many duties to my wife and kids. In fact, as a father of three kids, sometimes I feel like a professional Uber driver! I sacrifice *hours* of my weekly schedule (in the early morning, and late at night) driving my kids to practice, youth group, and other events. I am happy to do it and consider my family my *first* ministry. Yet Paul notes that married people have divided loyalties of pleasing their spouses *and* the Lord, whereas single people can wholeheartedly focus on pleasing the Lord (1 Cor. 7:32–35).

While single people do not have divided loyalty between their spouses and the Lord, singleness also comes with its own challenges. As a single pastor, Sam Allberry describes the temptation for single people to become self-centered when living alone. He notes how single people can do *what* they want, *when* they want to, and *however* they want to do it. They don't have anyone else to please. And yet he says, "We need to remind ourselves, daily, that our singleness is not for us but for the Lord."[2]

> Singleness and marriage are equal ways of serving the Lord. Both offer unique blessings, and both have unique challenges.

Here's the bottom line: Singleness and marriage are equal ways of serving the Lord. Both offer unique blessings, and both

---

[2] Sam Allberry, *7 Myths about Singleness* (Wheaton, IL: Crossway, 2019), 33.

have unique challenges. Whether single or married, we are each called to find our identity in Christ and to use our marital status in service to the Lord. Remember, our lives are not *ours*. We tend to approach life with the goal of getting the most out of it that we can. But if we focus on living for *Him*, then we don't have to worry about "missing out" on the things of this world.

Serve the Lord with Your Singleness

How can single people find the strength to serve the Lord? First, develop healthy relationships with God and other people. Second, cultivate the desire to live obediently to Jesus through spiritual disciplines and the power of the Holy Spirit. Third, look to Jesus as an example. Remember, Jesus was truly human. He was tempted in every way like us—including *sexual* temptation—and yet never sinned (Heb. 4:15). Jesus completely knows what single people go through in their daily temptations.

Quite insightfully, Todd Wilson observes: "No one was more fully human or sexually contented than Jesus, yet Jesus never engaged in a single sexual act."[3] Let that sink in. Although Jesus experienced sexual temptations, He never touched a woman inappropriately or indulged a single sexual fantasy. And yet He lived the most relationally satisfied life *ever*!

What this tells us, quite powerfully, is that sexual activity is not necessary for a meaningful and abundant life. Jesus found meaning through obedience to God and in loving, faithful relationships with

---

[3] Todd Wilson, *Mere Sexuality: Rediscovering the Christian Vision of Sexuality* (Grand Rapids, MI: Zondervan, 2017), 48–49.

family and friends. He was content in His sexuality as a single man even though He abstained from sex.

The life of Jesus portrays something utterly countercultural: *sex is not required for a flourishing life*. This was true when Jesus walked the earth and it is true today.

Singleness Foreshadows Heaven

In an earlier chapter on the purpose of sex, we saw that God intends sex to foreshadow heaven. The "one-flesh" union anticipates the ultimate fulfillment all believers will experience with God and others in heaven. Although in a different fashion, singleness also helps beautifully foreshadow heaven. Let me explain.

In Luke 20, some Sadducees question Jesus about the marital status of a woman who had married seven brothers, one at a time, after each had died: "In the resurrection, therefore, whose wife will the woman be? For the seven had her as wife" (v. 33). They are trying to show the absurdity of belief in a final resurrection.

But Jesus points out that there is no marriage in heaven. Thus, the woman won't be married to *any* of her former husbands, and certainly not *all* of them. The three purposes of sex—procreation, unity, and foreshadowing heaven—only apply to this present life. There will be no more procreation. There will be no need for the sexual bonding, because all people will be able to connect with God and other people in a deeper union. And we won't need sex to foreshadow heaven because we will be *in* heaven. Sex and marriage are for this life alone.

This is one reason why singleness is so important for the church today. Given that we will not be married in heaven, single people *in the present* help us look forward to the future resurrection when we are directly related to Christ and others. Single people *right now* anticipate our *future* eternal state. How so?

In her book *The Significance of Singleness*, Christina Hitchcock notes, "Relationships in the resurrection (God's future for his people) will not be characterized by marriage. Each person will be directly related to Christ, and all other relations will go through that first relationship in a way that we cannot fully understand now. . . . Marriage will become unnecessary and outmoded because all relationships will be fulfilled in and through Jesus. Singleness is a sign not of loneliness but of perfected community."[4]

The ultimate destiny for believers is a heavenly state of perfect community. Given that there will be no sin, fear, or shame, we will be able to love God and other people—which is what we were made *for*—without any limitations. We will no longer be tempted to believe that sexual experiences, or human relationships *alone*, can bring ultimate contentment.

Single people today play the vital role of reminding the church that ultimate satisfaction comes in the resurrection when we know God fully. Single people remind us that our ultimate satisfaction is found in marriage—but *not* marriage to a fellow human being of the opposite sex. Rather, our ultimate satisfaction comes from our heavenly marriage to Christ.

---

[4] Christina S. Hitchcock, *The Significance of Singleness* (Grand Rapids, MI: Baker, 2018), 33.

QUESTION

How do I make a good friend?

The world says you need sex, but what you need more deeply are healthy friendships. The place to start is to lay your request for a friend before the LORD (Ps. 37:4), and He will give you the desires of your heart. Specifically, what can you do? Either try to connect deeper with people you already know or join a team, club, or youth group to meet new people. Without being overbearing, take the initiative in the relationship and look for opportunities to connect. Seek common interests. Be loyal and trustworthy. Consider talking to a trusted leader for direction.

CHAPTER 16

Myth 1: Singleness Means No Family

I love my family deeply. While I enjoy the ministry aspect of teaching, speaking, and writing, a significant motivation in my efforts is to provide for my family. In fact, I often take red-eye flights home to minimize traveling time so I can be with my wife and kids *as soon as possible*! It is hard for me to imagine life without them.

This is one reason I have so much compassion for my single friends who wish they were married. Sure, some enjoy singleness and don't want to get married. But others want to be married, and for whatever reason, are not. Does this mean they don't have a family?

Answering this question begins with seeing how Jesus reconstitutes the nature of family from what is first portrayed in Genesis. As you will recall, God created humans as male and female and commanded them to multiply and fill the earth (Gen. 1:27–28). God designed human beings to fulfill this command through the natural family, which involves a man leaving his mother and father and bonding with his wife as a new family unit (Gen. 2:24).

Families grow into communities, communities grow into cities, and cities grow into nations, thus filling the earth. It all *begins* with the biological family. This is partly why the family was considered the primary social unit for the Hebrew people (*and* why childlessness was considered such a curse). Ultimately, God would redeem mankind by the fruitfulness and multiplication He commanded in the garden—a Savior would be born to a woman (Gen. 3:15; Gal. 4:4).

In the Old Testament, the family was central to God's plan for filling the earth and redeeming it. But in surprising fashion, Jesus transforms the nature of family in the New Testament.

In Matthew 12:46–50, the mother and brothers of Jesus stood outside where He was teaching and tried to get His attention. In response, Jesus stretched out His hand toward His disciples and said,

Jesus transforms the nature of family in the New Testament.

"Here are my mother and my brothers! For whoever does the will of my Father in heaven is my brother and sister and mother" (vv. 49–50).

Do you realize how *radical* this was? In a culture that grounded identity in the natural family, Jesus redrew family lines! Family status is not determined *horizontally* by the natural family, according to Jesus, but *vertically* based on a relationship with God. Simply put, brother and sister in Christ are now more important than brother and sister in the natural family.

Single people may not have a spouse, and most do not have biological children, yet along with married people, they are *equal* members of the family of God. And we must treat them that way.

What does this look like? In churches, this may mean not siphoning singles off into their own groups separated from the rest of the church. Some of my single friends feel that the emphasis in the church on married classes, groups, and teachings sends the unintended message that singles are second-class citizens. In families, this may mean building intentional relationships with single people and inviting them into the rhythms of life. One of my single friends is a godparent who regularly joins his married friends on vacation. In the church and in families, we must find creative ways to build healthy relationships with single people so they can flourish. They are a vital part of the family of God.

Does this mean it's easy to be single? This is the question we will explore in the next chapter.

>>————————→ **QUESTION** ←————————《

I am hurting from a past relationship. How long should I wait for another?

If you are hurting from a past relationship, I am sorry you are going through this. I know how much it can hurt. If you have regrets, know that God loves and forgives you (1 John 1:9). Because of the emotional pain after a broken relationship, there can be a strong temptation to "rebound" quickly to another. But this can be a mistake if you have not emotionally healed. Since your situation is unique, my advice is for you to go to a trusted adult—a parent, teacher, or pastor—who loves God and cares about you and seek their advice.

CHAPTER 17

Myth 2: Singleness Is Easy

To many young people, the single adult life can seem like a thrilling adventure. Go where you want. Eat what you want. Basically, do *what* you want, *when* you want to, and *however* you want to do it. You are the captain of your life.

As we discussed earlier, singleness offers greater freedom than marriage. And it offers a unique way of serving the church. But does that mean singleness is easy?

Some single people say yes. Such people tend to have rich friendships and relationships that give their lives meaning. But many people find the single life quite challenging.

Take Ed Shaw, for instance, a pastor who has embraced the life of singleness. While he has a wealth of great friends, he still describes "kitchen floor moments" of loneliness where he cries because of the "acute pain" of not having a partner, sex, children, and the rest.[1]

Consider another example. In his book *7 Myths about Singleness*, Sam Allberry describes the pain of seeing two of his closest friends move away the same summer. As a single man who deeply values friendship, he mourns the lack of commitment often associated with friendship. "People will move for family or economic reasons," he notes, "but no one moves for friends."[2]

How can singles find the strength to be faithful in the midst of these challenges? According to Shaw, what gets him off the kitchen floor is "embracing the truth that long-term happiness I long for comes through obedience to God's Word."[3] In other words, rather than accepting the cultural script, which proclaims sex and marriage as essential for happiness, Shaw looks to God and His Word for authority. Shaw trusts God, even though it is not easy.

Neither singleness nor marriage can bring lasting contentment.

According to Allberry, the key is the same for both single people and married people: *look to Christ for contentment.* Neither singleness nor marriage can bring lasting contentment. The key is not to make singleness or marriage into our source of contentment, but to look to Christ

---

[1] Ed Shaw, *Same-Sex Attraction and the Church* (Downers Grove, IL: InterVarsity Press, 2015), 61.
[2] Sam Allberry, *7 Myths about Singleness* (Wheaton, IL: Crossway, 2019), 136.
[3] Shaw, *Same-Sex Attraction and the Church*, 69.

regardless of our marital state. After all, Jesus said He is the "bread of life," and that whoever comes to Him will never hunger or thirst again (John 6:35).

There is so much the church can learn from people like Ed and Sam. Their commitment to faithfully serve God as single people, even though it is not easy, should inspire us all. As you may recall from chapter 2: *difficult things are meaningful. Nothing worth having comes easy.* Single people remind all of us of the importance of trusting God even when it is not easy.

Some people find singleness easy. But many single people find it difficult. This raises an important question: Is singleness *too* difficult for some people? Let's explore that question in the next chapter.

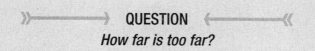

QUESTION
How far is too far?

Rather than giving you a specific line, consider a biblical principle. Philippians 4:8 says to think about pure, lovely, and honorable things. You should be asking not how far you can go, but how to treat a date with love and honor as someone with whom you have no marriage covenant. Can you hold hands with that person and think thoughts that are pure? Sure. Can you hug and think honorable thoughts? Probably. Kissing? Well, maybe. Sexual touching? No chance. Clearly there is a point of physical contact where your thoughts will shift from honoring and loving the other to desiring increased illicit sexual contact. *That* is a good indication you have gone too far.

CHAPTER 18

Myth 3: Singleness Is Too Difficult

In the last chapter, we saw that it is a mistake to think that singleness is easy. But it is also a mistake to view singleness as too difficult.

In Matthew 19:3–12, the Pharisees ask Jesus about divorce. He answers by quoting Genesis 1:27 and 2:24, which affirm that God intends marriage to be the union of one man and one woman *for life*. According to Jesus, the "one-flesh" union of marriage is meant to be permanent, which is why He then says, "And I say to you: whoever divorces his wife, except for sexual immorality, and marries another, commits adultery" (v. 9).

Quite obviously, Jesus holds a high view of marriage! In fact, His disciples are so startled by His radical teaching they conclude, "If such is the case of a man with his wife, it is better not to marry" (v. 10). The disciples didn't struggle with thinking singleness was too difficult; in light of the high view Jesus held of marriage, they thought marriage might be too difficult!

Given the high commitment of marriage, Jesus seems to imply that some people should remain single. If you are not prepared to embrace the lifelong, permanent commitment of marriage, then you should remain single. Jesus considered marriage a difficult calling.

Ironically, many people today view singleness and marriage in the opposite fashion. Rather than viewing marriage as too difficult for some to embrace, many people today view singleness as the more difficult road. Singleness is now considered hard (often because of the lack of sexual activity), and marriage is considered easy.

But here's the reality: both marriage and singleness can be difficult. Even though the challenges of marriage and singleness are different, neither marriage *nor* singleness is easy. Neither are they too difficult.

Given the difficulty of being sexually pure, did Jesus soften His commands to accommodate single people? No, in fact Jesus *raised* the expectations of sexual purity for *all His followers*. He taught that sex should be reserved for one man and one woman in marriage, that all kinds of sexual immorality are wrong (Mark 7:21), and that sexual immorality includes lustful thoughts (Matt. 5:27–28). This is a high bar!

While Jesus did not experience sexual intimacy, He did experience relational intimacy.

How can a single person (either for a season or for life) be expected to follow such difficult commands? First, Jesus modeled such faithfulness Himself. Jesus was truly human like us and He remained sexually pure. Jesus does not call us, His followers, to do anything He did not accomplish Himself.

Second, while Jesus did not experience sexual intimacy, He did experience *relational intimacy*. Even though He was a virgin, Jesus lived a fully flourishing life through intimate relationships with God the Father, with His family, and with His friends. Jesus calls us to experience the same kind of relational intimacy with others.

Third, Jesus sent the Holy Spirit to help us fight against the passions of the flesh (Gal. 5:16–25). He convicts us of sin and temptation, points us to the cross in times of need, and assures us of God's love and forgiveness.

And finally, when we fall short, God is there to forgive us, restore us, and set us back on the right path.

Yes, singleness can be difficult. And marriage can be difficult too. But neither is *too* difficult. Many young people today attest to this with their very own lives. Although they are a minority, many young Christians today reject the worldly narrative about sex and embrace the radical call of Jesus. My hope is that this group includes *you*.

Yes, this road can be difficult. But remember, God's grace is sufficient for you.

QUESTION
Is it okay to date a nonbeliever?

Second Corinthians 6:14 helps with this question: "Do not be unequally yoked with unbelievers." While this command is given in the context of not associating with pagan practices, it carries the wider connotation that Christians need to be very careful "harnessing" themselves too closely with spiritual opposites. While not all Christians would be good to date, and many non-Christians are caring and respectful, it is unwise to date someone who does not share your deepest faith convictions. Doing so can create a tension between pleasing your date and honoring God, which is why the Bible says to guard your heart (Prov. 4:23).

CHAPTER 19

The Purpose of Marriage

Even though it was released a number of years ago, *The Notebook* continues to be a popular romantic film today. Ryan Gosling and Rachel McAdams star as a young couple who fall in love in the 1940s. An elderly man, played by the late James Garner, reads the story of these two lovers from his notebook to a woman in a present-day nursing home. At the end, we discover that the woman is his wife. Although she has dementia, the story triggers her memory, and the couple die in one another's arms with one final memory of their love.

The Notebook is a heart-rending story. My daughter loved it. It contains many redeeming elements, such as the idea of keeping a marriage commitment *in sickness and in health.*

But the movie also contains some questionable ideas about the nature of marriage that should give thoughtful Christians pause. For instance, the movie depicts a "soul mate" view of marriage in which marriage is primarily characterized by the deep emotional intensity two people have for one another. If you can just find such a partner—your *soul mate*—then your life will be filled with passion and meaning. On this view, marriage is not about procreation, parenting, or building society, but about finding that *one* romantic partner you were destined to be with. *Then* you can be happy.

Is this a realistic view of marriage?

We resonate with *The Notebook* because we want to experience deep, abiding love. But here is the question: Should we expect love to swoop us up, like the gust of emotional intensity depicted in *The Notebook*, and carry us passionately through life? Marriage undoubtedly involves passion. I love my wife dearly and we are passionate about our relationship with one another. But the reality is that if we relied upon the unrealistic level of emotional intensity depicted in *The Notebook*, we would have shipwrecked our marriage a long time ago.

A harmful implication of *The Notebook*'s vision of marriage is that if your life isn't filled with passion and meaning, your spouse must not truly be your soul mate. If you don't feel love for your spouse, so the thinking goes, you must've picked the wrong one. Time to go looking for another. The result is a lot of shipwrecked marriages.

But here's the reality: marriage involves times when you may not *feel* love for your spouse. If you want a deep, abiding marriage, you *choose* to love your spouse regardless of how you feel. Weaving together two different lives into a coherent story takes time, work, and effort. Trust me, it doesn't happen by itself. But when we commit to loving each other *regardless of how we feel,* we put ourselves in a position to build a lasting, meaningful marriage that fulfills God's deeper purpose for marriage.

If marriage is not about finding your soul mate, then what *is* its purpose? The best way to answer this question is to go back to God's original design for marriage (as we did for sex). After all, God is the one who invented marriage in the first place. Thus, the best way to know what to expect in marriage is to ask the question, "What is marriage *for*?"

And this takes us back to Genesis. Let's consider two vital passages for understanding the purpose of marriage:

> So God created man in his own image, in the image of God he created him; male and female he created them. And God blessed them. And God said to them, "Be fruitful and multiply and fill the earth and subdue it." (Gen. 1:27–28a)

> Therefore a man shall leave his father and his mother and hold fast to his wife, and they shall become one flesh. (Gen. 2:24)

These passages offer seven important insights about the nature of marriage.

Marriage Involves Partners of Equal Value

In stark contrast to other ancient creation stories, the Bible considers women to have equal value to men. Do you realize how radical this was in the ancient world? The Bible begins with the proclamation that *both* men and women are equal image-bearers of God. Eve is described as being Adam's helper (*ezer*), but this does not imply inferiority. In fact, God is often described as our *ezer* (e.g., Ps. 30:10).

Marriage Is Meant to Be Permanent

The man is to leave his father and mother and "hold fast" to his wife. The Hebrew word for hold (*dabaq*) carries the idea of joining, bonding, and sticking together *as one*.

By the way, this idea of permanence is not imposed on love by the Bible. As human beings we yearn for permanent love. Song after song today proclaims a love that is meant to last forever. The desire for permanent love is written on our hearts and described in the early chapter of Genesis.

Marriage Is a Sexually Complementary Institution

According to Genesis, God designed males and females as complements of one another. Men and women share common humanity but differ in their biological sex. Marriage is not an institution of *any* two people, but of two *opposite*-sexed people.

Marriage Is about Procreation

As we have seen, God designed sex to be experienced in the context of marriage. Thus, a key purpose of marriage is procreation. Marriage is the institution God designed to "multiply and fill the earth."

Marriage Is about Companionship

Genesis describes the married couple as becoming "one flesh," which means they become one spiritually, physically, emotionally, *and* relationally. Marriage is a comprehensive union that includes a relational dimension. Later stories in Genesis, such as Abraham and Sarah, Isaac and Rebekah, and Jacob and Rachel support the idea that marriage involves deep companionship.

Marriage Is Meant to Be Monogamous

The man is meant to leave his father and mother and "hold fast to his wife." The man leaves a household involving a mother and a father, and then he creates a household with his wife. Even though Old Testament figures often took many wives, and failed to live this ideal, God's intent from the beginning has been that marriage involves one man and one woman.

Marriage Is Good

As we saw earlier, procreation was not a result of the fall, but part of God's good creation. The same is true for marriage. Although there is much hurt and brokenness in how people experience marriage today, God has deemed marriage "very good" (Gen. 1:31) since the beginning.

These seven insights are vital for understanding what God originally designed marriage *for*. But this is only the beginning of the story. Marriage serves three specific purposes in both society and the church.

First, *God designed marriage to portray His love for the church.* In the Old Testament, marriage is a metaphor describing God's relationship to Israel. God did not merely have a legal contract with Israel, but He created a loving covenant with them that was depicted through marriage. This is why Israel's unfaithfulness to God is often compared to adultery (for example, see Jer. 3:6–8).

Yet in the New Testament era, marriage between a husband and wife serves to depict Christ and His love for the church. The union of a man and a woman depict the *greater* union of Christ and His followers. The apostle Paul explains:

> "Therefore a man shall leave his father and mother and hold fast to his wife, and the two shall become one flesh." This mystery is profound, and I am saying that it refers to Christ and the church. (Eph. 5:31–32)

Can you see why faithfulness in marriage is so important? Unfaithful marriages—especially in the church—distort how people understand Christ's faithful love for the church. They preach a false gospel.

Second, *God designed marriage to portray His relational character.* While Christians believe in one God, we also believe that God exists as three distinct persons: Father, Son, and Holy Spirit. While there is *one* God in being, there are three *persons* who share the divine nature. As the Father, Son, and Holy Spirit, God is a relational being in His very nature.

Do you see how this relates to marriage? In marriage, two distinct *persons* become *one* family unit. There are distinct persons—husband and wife—who come together in relational unity. Remember,

God says in Genesis 2:24, "They shall become one flesh." The two persons ("They") become one family unit ("one flesh"). The relational nature of marriage reflects the relational character of God.

Again, can you see why it is so important for husbands and wives to sacrificially love each other? Marriage helps portray God's relational character.

Third, *God designed marriage for the flourishing of children and the benefit of society.* Although it is politically incorrect to say today, the truth is that kids do best when they live in a home with a mom and dad who love each other. Kids from such homes are less likely to drop out of school, abuse drugs and alcohol, attempt suicide, and become poor. Children without a mom and dad in the home are at increased risk for health, academic, emotional, and behavioral problems. There are certainly individuals who buck this trend, but the overall evidence is clear: kids do best in a home with a mom and a dad who love each other.

Marriage is not about finding your soul mate as the secret to a meaningful life. Marriage is about something much bigger.

Part of the role of government is to foster a healthy society. Since kids do best with a mom and a dad, the government should be interested in supporting a monogamous, lifelong vision of marriage.

For years, sociologists believed that the relationship with the mom was more vital for children than the connection with the father. Now we know that both matter deeply. In his book for

Scientific American, Paul Raeburn says, "Enough is known about the positive impact of fathers' presence on children's lives that governments should start changing public policies to encourage fathers to spend time with their children."[1] Yes!

Here is the bottom line about marriage. Are you ready? *Marriage is not about you.* Despite the message of *The Notebook*, marriage is not about finding your soul mate as the secret to a meaningful life. Marriage is about something much bigger. It is about sacrificing for your spouse and kids, as well as portraying God's loving character to the church and the wider world.

Again, marriage is not about you. And it is not about me. Marriage is about God's kingdom. When you and your spouse commit your marriage to *this* greater purpose, you will experience the beauty and richness of marriage as God designed it to be experienced.

---

[1] Paul Raeburn, *Do Fathers Matter? What Science Is Telling Us About the Parent We've Overlooked* (New York: Scientific American, 2014), 151.

》————→ **QUESTION** ←————《

Is abortion a valid form of birth control?

Birth control is meant to *prevent* pregnancy. Abortion, on the other hand, takes the life of an unborn human being and *ends* an existing pregnancy. The science is clear: a human being, who is distinct from the mother, emerges at conception. Thus, abortion should not be used as birth control because it involves taking the life of an innocent human being. If you find yourself pregnant, or have a friend who gets pregnant, please talk to a trusted adult or visit a pregnancy resource center. There *is* a better way than abortion. Adoption can be a beautiful way of blessing another family with a priceless gift.

CHAPTER 20

Myth 1: Marriage Will Fulfill Your Ultimate Relational Needs

A number of years ago I worked at a church in the inner city of Los Angeles. One of the youth ministers told me that when he first got married, he was hoping it would bring meaning and fulfillment to his life.

While he loved being married, it didn't work out as he anticipated, but then he thought it might happen when they had kids. Again, it didn't.

But then he said to me when he learned his wife was pregnant a second time, "I think a second child will do the trick."

What never seemed to cross his mind was the question of whether or not he should be looking to his marriage and family to fulfill his ultimate relational needs in the first place. Where did he get this idea? Certainly not in the Bible. Rather, he had seemingly bought the "soul mate" idea we discussed in the last chapter. Like Morpheus in *The Matrix*, he was looking for "the one" who would fill his deepest relational needs and desires. And when she didn't, he then moved on to his kids. And then what?

Let me ask you a question: If you get married someday, do you want your spouse looking to *you* to fulfill their greatest relational needs? I hope not. As Christopher West has observed, "If we look to another human person as our ultimate fulfillment, we will crush that person."[1]

As I have mentioned before, I am blessed with an amazing wife. We have a wonderful time together and provide deep relational meaning for each other. And I love my kids. But we also look *beyond* our immediate family to God, the church, and personal friends for our ultimate relational fulfillment.

In reality, many married couples experience loneliness. While there can be a range of reasons for this, one contributing factor is that some people enter into marriage *expecting* it to fulfill their greatest relational needs, and as a result, fail to cultivate other important relationships. Given their disappointment, some leave their marriages hoping to find their real "soul mate."

Marriage can fulfill *some* relational needs, but it is not meant to fulfill *all* our relational needs.

Marriage can fulfill *some* relational needs, but it is not meant to fulfill *all* our relational needs. Even King David understood the power of friendship, "I am distressed for you, my

---

[1] Christopher West, *Theology of the Body: Rediscovering the Meaning of Life, Love, Sex, and Gender* (North Palm Beach, FL: Wellspring, 2018), 102.

brother Jonathan; very pleasant have you been to me; your love to me was extraordinary, surpassing the love of women" (2 Sam. 1:26).

The Bible has a lot to say about the importance of friendship. For instance, Proverbs speaks of a friend who loves at all times (17:17), a friend who sticks closer than a brother (18:24), a friend who encourages righteousness (12:26), and the value of a friend who speaks truth (27:5–6).

Remember, Jesus was never married on Earth, but He lived the most relationally fulfilled life ever. He was single, and yet He had intimate relationships with God, His friends, and His disciples. Here is the bottom line: marriage is one powerful way of experiencing relational intimacy, but it is not the only way. Whether single or married, God designed *all* of us to develop friendships with others in the body of Christ.

>>————————→ **QUESTION** ←————————<<

*What should I do if someone is pressuring me
for nude pictures of myself?*

If someone is pressuring you to send nude pictures of yourself,
don't do it. You can say no. Not only is it wrong to send nude
pics—because your body belongs to the Lord and not to the
person asking you—but it is unwise and illegal. Many boys
who receive pictures of sexual images share them with others. You might intend an image for his eyes only, but once it is
sent, it is out there *forever* and can have devastating emotional
consequences. Sending nude pictures is illegal and considered
trafficking in child pornography. Some young people have been
hit with serious charges, such as being labeled sex offenders,
for sending and receiving sexual images on their smartphones.

CHAPTER 21

Myth 2: Marriage Will Get Rid of Your Sin

Anumber of years ago, I met a young man who habitually looked at pornography before he got married. While he kept it a secret, he was convinced that when he experienced "the real thing" in marriage, his porn habit would subside. He married a beautiful young woman, inside and out, but was surprised to learn that his porn habit continued shortly after their wedding night. In fact, it seemed to get worse.

When she discovered his habit, she instantly blamed herself. But the reality is that it was not *her* lack of attractiveness or beauty, but the stronghold that sin had over *his* life. She was not the one with the problem. He was. And unbeknownst to her, he brought this issue right into their marriage.

Not only did marriage not get rid of his sin, it seemed to make it worse it because it affected her more directly than it had before.

Sadly, this marriage ended in divorce. Trust was broken. The wounds ran too deep. They simply couldn't mend the marriage. He told me he wished more than anything that he could go back to high school and commit to sexual purity. From his perspective, had he confessed and experienced God's grace and healing as a young man, it might have saved his future marriage.

But not all such marriages end this way (and by the way, this young man has since experienced God's grace and healing in his life and moved on relationally). I have seen many broken marriages experience transformation when spouses work through a period of confession, accountability, and renewed commitment. God can heal even the most shattered marriages.

Here is the bottom line: marriage does not magically rid people of their sin. If you expect marriage to remove your selfishness, greed, pride, or lust, you are going to be disappointed. You are a sinner *before* you get married, and you will continue to be a sinner *after* you get married (1 John 1:8). And you will be a sinner your whole life even if you remain single. We bring our sinful selves into all our relationships, including marriage.

We bring our sinful selves into all our relationships, including marriage.

This is not an excuse for sin, but a recognition of why marriage can be so difficult. Although the Holy Spirit transforms believers to be more like Christ *in this life*, our sinful nature continues to plague us *until the next life*.

When there is confession, honesty, and grace, marriage can be a powerful place for healing and spiritual growth. But marriage alone will not automatically get rid of your sin. Expecting it to do so will only lead to disappointment.

QUESTION

What about anal sex?

To avoid pregnancy, or because of pressure, some young people engage in anal sex. First of all, it should be clear that this is well beyond the scope of what might be considered acceptable or pure for a dating couple. It is *not* okay. Second, you do not *have* to engage in any kind of sexual activity with someone who pressures you. You *can* and should say no. Further, our human anatomy and the very slight chance of pregnancy tells us that anal sex is risky, unsafe, and unwise.

CHAPTER 22

Myth 3: Married Sex Is Boring

One of the most common ideas about sex in our culture is that married sex is boring. In a question-and-answer session at a youth group, I remember a young man asking me how married sex could be enjoyable because, he asked, isn't variety the spice of life? How could sex with the same person for life *not eventually become boring*? If the same meal every night would eventually get boring, then why wouldn't sex with the same person eventually become boring too? Wouldn't more partners make someone happier?

On this view, married sex is considered boring since it involves commitment to one person for life.

Is this true? Is God's design for sex boring?

Quite remarkably, a recent study challenges the "variety" notion that happiness increases with more sexual partners.[1] The author

---

[1] Olga Khazan, "Fewer Sexual Partners Means a Happier Marriage," *The Atlantic* (October 22), 2018; https://www.theatlantic.com/health/archive/2018/10/sexual-partners-and-marital-happiness/573493/ (accessed November 18, 2019).

of the study found that two-thirds of women and 72 percent of men with one lifetime sexual partner reported being "very happy" with their marriage. The numbers dropped significantly with each increased sexual partner.

In other words, the *more* sexual partners someone had over the course of their life, the *less* satisfied they reported being in their marriage.

The point is not that premarital sex always feels bad. The Prodigal Son engaged in "wild living" and apparently enjoyed his life for a season. And the point is not that married sex is always fun. The point is that the "Hugh Hefner" narrative that "variety is the spice of life" is not only incomplete, it's harmful. Choosing to be sexually active before marriage doesn't ruin you for life. It doesn't mean you're damaged goods. As we've already said, God's grace in Christ is sufficient for every kind of sin. But the reality is, if you choose to be sexually active before marriage, you do put the quality of your future marriage at risk.

In the chapter on the purpose of sex, we saw that God's design for sex, despite claims to the contrary, offers the greatest sexual freedom. This is not a freedom to have sex with an endless array of partners, but the kind of freedom found only in commitment. Sex according to God's design offers freedom from comparison, and freedom from the fear that comes along with contracting a sexually transmitted infection. It offers the freedom to love, and be loved, without shame.

A strong case can actually be made that married people, who follow God's design for sex, are having the *most* and the *best* sex.[2]

---

[2] See Sean McDowell and Jonathan Morrow, *Is God Just a Human Invention?* (Grand Rapids, MI: Kregel, 2010), 185–94.

And there are good reasons for this. However, my point is not to convince you to be sexually pure so that you can have the best sex in marriage. We should be motivated toward sexual purity out of a desire to honor God and love other people. We are called to be holy because God is holy (1 Pet. 1:16).

We should be motivated toward sexual purity out of a desire to honor God and love other people. We are called to be holy because God is holy.

The popular claim that married sex is boring is a myth. *Some* married sex may be boring, but certainly not *most* married sex. When my father was seventy-four years old, a teenager asked him when sex stops being enjoyable. Without hesitation, my dad replied, "I don't know, but I do know for sure that it is some time after seventy-four!"

God is the one who designed sex to be pleasurable in the first place (Prov. 5:19; Song of Solomon). He is the one who gave us sex as a blessing and a gift. Doesn't it make sense to listen to Him?

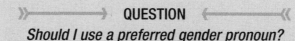

QUESTION

Should I use a preferred gender pronoun?

Christians are divided on this difficult question. Let's consider both sides. Those who support using preferred pronouns emphasize the importance of the relationship. In the eyes of many people who are transgender, not using their preferred pronoun means you do not truly care about them. Thus, using a preferred pronoun is being charitable. Those opposed to using preferred pronouns emphasize the power of words. Since people cannot biologically switch sexes, preferred pronouns affirm a false reality, and thus distort truth. It potentially brings harm to your conscience, the individual, and the wider society. Wrestle through this question with friends and a trusted adult.

PART 3

CHAPTER 23

Pornography

Not long ago, I met a young man at a church conference who had married his high school sweetheart. As a high school and college student, unbeknownst to her, he began habitually looking at pornography. Even though he *knew* it was wrong, he kept it a secret, convinced he would shed the habit when he got married.

His habit stopped the first few weeks of their marriage, but when stress set in, and he lacked a healthy way to cope with it, he reverted back to viewing porn. When his wife inadvertently discovered it, her trust in him was shattered, and they were divorced soon thereafter. I will never forget him sharing how he wished—more than anything—that he could go back to high school and listen to the messages he heard about God's design for sex and marriage. If so, he told me, his marriage may have turned out differently.

I realize this is a dramatic story. My point is not to scare you or to make you feel particularly shameful if you struggle with porn, but to *motivate* you to take the issue seriously in your life *now*. Please don't wait.

As a speaker and teacher, I hear countless heartbreaking stories of relationships destroyed by pornography. Research indicates that porn use even contributes to many young Christians leaving their faith.[1] Quite obviously, in a book on sex, love, and relationships, we *need* to talk about pornography.

Here is the sobering reality today that *breaks my heart*: Your generation is growing up with more access to porn than any previous generation. More people today—including men, women *and* children—regularly watch porn than ever before in history. And this is utterly transforming how people think about sex, love, and relationships.

We need to be especially careful to build our worldview from Scripture rather than the lies that emanate from our pornified culture. Let's consider three of the biggest myths propagated today about pornography.

Myth 1: "It Doesn't Affect Me."

A number of years ago when I was teaching high school Bible, a student shared with me about how he had been habitually looking at porn late into the night, and he was unsure what to do about it.

Before walking with him through the issue, I simply asked how viewing pornography affected him *personally*. He gave the same answer I hear all the time from young men who look at porn: he had a hard time looking at a woman without viewing her as a sex object. Without realizing it, watching porn conditioned him to view women as *things* to be used for pleasure rather than as human beings to be valued and loved.

---

[1] Samuel L. Perry, *Addicted to Lust: Pornography in the Lives of Conservative Protestants* (New York: Oxford University Press, 2019), 76–87.

Pornography shapes the worldview of those who watch it, and this is especially true for young men *and* young women who lack the wisdom and context to process their experience. Here is the bottom line: whether you realize it or not, watching pornography unrealistically shapes your sexual expectations, preferences, and practices regarding sex. For instance, porn depicts sex outside marriage as exciting, which subtly (but powerfully) encourages you to feel it is okay. Also, watching porn prompts you to accept the false impression that "everyone is doing it."

Whether you realize it or not, watching pornography unrealistically shapes your sexual expectations, preferences, and practices regarding sex.

According to a massive study on the impact of internet pornography on adolescents, if you view pornography, you are more likely to engage in sexual harassment, have insecurities about your sexual abilities and body image, have clinical symptoms of depression, be distracted by thoughts of sex, engage in sexually permissive behavior, and a number of other negative outcomes.[2]

"It doesn't affect me." Myth.

---

[2] Eric W. Owens, Richard J. Behun, Jill C. Manning, and Rory C. Reid, "The Impact of Pornography on Adolescents: A Review of the Research," in *Sexual Addiction & Compulsivity,* Vol. 19 (2012), 99–122.

Myth 2: "I Will Quit Later."

When I was in elementary school, my father led a national campaign on sexual purity. After one of his lectures, a lady approached him for counsel. She shared how her husband could not be sexually intimate with her without having a *Playboy* magazine on the pillow next to her head. Heartbroken, she asked my father for advice.

Even though I was young, I remember feeling sad for her. Why did her husband "need" a *Playboy*? The answer is revealing: he had re-wired his brain through habitual porn use to respond sexually to an image rather than to a real person. Sadly, he couldn't fully love his wife *as his wife* without bringing pornography into their relationship—which is to say, he wasn't loving his wife at all.

Few people realize how deeply porn rewires the brain and thus shapes human behavior. The younger someone is, the more looking at porn shapes the development of his or her brain, which can have a lifelong impact. Research shows that it is far easier to quit gambling, alcohol addiction, heroin, and cocaine than porn. Why? Because of what it does to your brain.[3]

Consider the neurochemical dopamine, which can make a person feel good when engaging in exciting behavior, such as riding a roller coaster. Because dopamine creates such a powerful feeling of exhilaration, people naturally seek more of the behavior that caused its release. While dopamine serves an important function in how we feel pleasure, it can also be abused. Drugs like heroin, cocaine, and even marijuana cause a powerful release of dopamine, which satisfies the biological reward system in a big way. Yet it also raises

---

[3] "The Porn Epidemic," Josh McDowell Ministry; josh.org/resources/apologetics/research/#pornportfolio.

the threshold for this kind of pleasure, which generates the craving of more drugs to get the same high, and fosters addiction.

Viewing pornography and being sexually active *also* cause dopamine release. Thus, the same neurochemical that drives addiction in certain drugs is released when viewing porn. Like certain drugs, porn also raises the threshold for experiencing pleasure through dopamine. Yet unlike drugs, the "solution" is not *more* pornography, but greater *variety*.

This is one reason porn can be so addictive. To get the same "high," porn fosters the desire for greater and greater variety, which often leads down a more twisted and broken, more violent and even illegal, path. Can you see why it is so naïve to flippantly assume you can control it? The brain is simply not built that way.

"I will quit later." Myth.

Myth 3: "I Am Not Harming Anyone."

This myth is getting tougher to defend. Here's why.

Pornography harms performers. Thousands of ex-performers have come forward to share their stories of the dark side of the porn industry. Former female performers tell stories of verbal, physical, and sexual abuse. Former male performers describe the porn industry as involving violence, drugs, and disease.[4]

Porn harms marriages. You may be tempted to think that looking at porn might spice up a relationship. Yet the opposite is true:

---

[4] For instance, see Fight the New Drug, "5 Male Ex-Performers Share What It's Really Like to Do Porn" (September 3, 2019); https://fightthe newdrug.org/3-male-porn-stars-share-their-most-disturbing-experiences -doing-porn/.

marriages suffer when porn is involved. Multiple studies reveal that viewing porn decreases satisfaction in a marriage as well as commitment and faithfulness. Spouses who look at porn are habituated to think the grass is greener elsewhere, and as a result, undermine the health of their marriage.[5]

Porn harms children. Because their brains are still developing, the healthy development of children is especially compromised by the destructive messages of porn.[6] Sadly, there is a trend of children sexually abusing other children by acting out pornographic sex scenes.

Porn sites make money through advertising. The more page views they get, the more money companies will pay them to advertise at their site. Even browsing a porn site contributes to its profits. Here's the bottom line: viewing porn helps line the pockets of porn companies. Thus, if you browse porn sites (even without paying), you are contributing to the harm they cause.

"I am not harming anyone." Sorry, that's also a myth.

Avoiding the Snare of Pornography

In closing, let me suggest a few practical steps for avoiding the snare of pornography.

---

[5] John D. Foubert, *How Pornography Harms* (Bloomington, IN: LifeRich Publishing, 2017), 63–64.

[6] See Allison Baxter, "How Pornography Harms Children: The Advocates Role," *The American Bar Association* (May 1, 2014); https://www.americanbar.org/groups/public_interest/child_law/resources/child_law_practiceonline/child_law_practice/vol-33/may-2014/how-pornography-harms-children--the-advocate-s-role/.

First, get a filter on your various devices. If you're tempted to use loopholes to try to get around filters, find the most rigorous software available. This is a practical, natural way to build accountability into your life.[7]

Second, confess your sins to a fellow Christian and experience God's grace. Burying sin can create a cycle of guilt and shame, but confessing sin brings freedom (see 2 Cor. 4:2). Share your struggles with a trusted adult and allow him or her to encourage you with God's grace and forgiveness. Simply talking through your temptations and failures, and experiencing acceptance and grace, can help set you free from the lure of pornography.

Third, understand that porn use is a symptom of a deeper brokenness. If you have past hurts, they could be fueling your habit. Remember, God designed us to experience healthy relationships with Him *and* with other people. Pornography aims to fill the good desire God has given us with a relational counterfeit. Addressing habitual porn use *must* begin with the goal of becoming relationally healthy through building intimate connections with God and other people.

And when we are relationally healthy, we become empowered to truly love others.

---

[7] While there are some wonderful ministries that can help, I personally recommend Covenant Eyes; www.covenanteyes.com.

> → **QUESTION** ←
> *Is masturbation okay?*
>
> While Christians differ on the morality of masturbation, all can agree that lust is wrong (see Matt. 5:27–29). Some consider masturbation acceptable if it is done with a spouse and without sinful sexual fantasy. Yet, when masturbation is done in secret, it can condition someone to experience sexual release alone, and potentially bring dysfunction into a future marriage. Further, lust-free masturbation in any other context than with a spouse seems almost impossible. Since it involves the release of dopamine, masturbation can also be highly addictive. With the help of the Holy Spirit, healthy accountability, and a large dose of grace, you should foster self-control in this area of your life.

CHAPTER 24

Cohabitation

Would living with someone before marriage help or hurt that marriage? What do *you* think?

Over the years, I have engaged thousands of high school students in conversation about the wisdom of living together before marriage. Typically, I begin a class discussion by writing two columns on the board. One is for the *positive* effects of cohabitation and the other is for the *negative* effects. Then, regardless of their personal beliefs, I have them fill in both columns as thoroughly as they can.

And then the discussion begins.

As you can imagine, students have a range of views on the issue. At this stage, the goal is simply to get them debating the merits of cohabitation. Then after a short while, I put the following provocative (and true) statement on the board: "Couples with cohabiting experience are between 50 and 80 percent more likely to divorce than couples with no such experience." Then I ask, "Why do you think this is the case?"

Students tend to find this fact both surprising *and* difficult to believe. After all, it seems obvious that living with someone first would help ensure a successful marriage. And yet the research is so clear about the damaging effects of cohabitation that Glenn Stanton, author of *The Ring Makes All the Difference*, concludes, "If couples want to *increase* to a near certainty their likelihood of divorcing once they do marry, there are few things more widely practiced that could accomplish this more efficiently than living together before marriage."[1]

Couples with cohabiting experience are between 50 and 80 percent more likely to divorce than couples with no such experience.

Given how much society emphasizes nonjudgmentalism toward cohabiting relationships, you might be tempted to dismiss the data about their ineffectiveness as a fluke, an aberration. You might also be tempted to think that you could be an exception to the rule. But this would be a huge mistake. There is scant evidence that cohabitation benefits a couple.[2] And there is a *wealth* of research indicating the harm cohabitation often brings to both couples and children.

Consider a few statistics about how cohabiting relationships compare with marital relationships:

---

[1] Glenn T. Stanton, *The Ring Makes All the Difference* (Chicago, IL: Moody, 2011), 64.

[2] Scott Stanley, "Premarital Cohabitation Is Still Associated with Greater Odds of Divorce," *Institute for Family Studies* (Oct. 17, 2018); https://ifstudies.org/blog/premarital-cohabitation-is-still-associated-with-greater-odds-of-divorce/.

- Cohabitors are twice as likely to report domestic violence.
- Cohabitors are much more likely to cheat on their partner.
- Cohabitors have lower earnings and savings.
- Cohabiting men are less likely to help with chores around the house.
- Cohabiting men are more likely to engage in high-risk behavior such as being out too late at bars or driving too fast.
- Cohabitors experience more disagreements and fights.[3]

Simply put, cohabitors are far less likely to have a healthy relationship in comparison with married couples on *all* important measures. And perhaps most tragic, in comparison with children living with their married parents, children with cohabiting parents are more likely to end up in poverty, more likely to have academic and behavioral problems, and more likely to experience physical, emotional, and sexual abuse.[4]

If the research is so unfavorable toward cohabitation—and it *is*—why would anyone choose it?

One reason might be that some people are simply unaware of the negative effects of living together before marriage. Many people in my generation (known as Generation X) experienced pain, alienation, and disillusionment when their parents divorced. Not wanting their kids to experience the same hurt, they chose cohabitation

---

[3] Stanton, *The Ring Makes All the Difference*, 44–51.
[4] Ibid., 79–84.

with their next partner, hoping it would improve their chances of marital success. Despite their good intentions, their choice has often had the reverse effect.

There is a second surprising reason many couples cohabit: they *slide* into it. In his extensive research on cohabitation, researcher Scott Stanley demonstrated that more than half of couples living together did not make a deliberate *decision* to do so. Thus, he coined the term, "sliding vs. deciding," to indicate that a majority of cohabitors moved in together without giving it much thought or reflection.[5]

After college, my wife and I both worked in Southern California. She was teaching high school and I was working at an inner-city church in Hollywood. To save money, time, and hassle, it would have been easy to *slide* into cohabitation. Instead, we rented separate apartments in the same complex because we *decided* not to live together until marriage. Would it have been easy to move in together and save a few thousand dollars? Sure. But do I regret it? Not for a second. To give ourselves the best chance of marital success, we made the intentional *decision* to live separately until marriage.

Please recognize how deeply the decisions you make now will shape your future marriage. This is true for a range of issues, and *especially* for the decision of whether or not to cohabitate. If you want to have a happy, fulfilling, and lasting marriage, one of the most important decisions you can make is to refrain from moving in with your future spouse before tying the knot.

---

[5] Scott Stanley, https://slidingvsdeciding.blogspot.com/. His extensive research and documentation can be found at this site.

There are three primary reasons cohabitation jeopardizes successful marriages:

First, while cohabitation and marriage both involve sharing resources, living space, and sexual activity, they are fundamentally different *kinds* of relationships. The core ingredient that makes marriage work—categorical commitment to one's spouse—is absent in cohabitation. Even if cohabiting couples *believe* their relationship is akin to marriage, without the public commitment, wedding license, and wedding rings, they are less obliged to the success of the relationship. They are freer to walk away. And as a result, the relationship suffers.

Cohabiting couples may be physically *together*, but this is not the same as being categorically *committed* to one another. Married couples consistently report higher levels of relational satisfaction, closeness to their partner, and trust.[6] Why? The answer is simple: commitment.

This is especially true for women. A woman needs the safety and security of knowing a man will not abandon her if she becomes pregnant. She needs to know the man will commit to caring for her and their children *no matter what*. With this

> The core ingredient that makes marriage work—categorical commitment to one's spouse—is absent in cohabitation.

---

[6] Belinda Luscombe, "More People Think It's Fine for Unwed Couples to Live Together. Here's Why Many Still Think Marriage Is Better," *Time magazine* (Nov. 6, 2019); https://time.com/5718695/marriage-living-together-pew-research/.

commitment in place, a married couple is free to experience a deep level of relational satisfaction unavailable to those who simply live together.

Second, men and women tend to have the same expectations of permanency in marriage, which is expressed in marital vows to love one another "in sickness and in health." But in cohabiting relationships, men and women tend to have different expectations, which often lead to conflict and disappointment.

Men tend to view cohabiting relationships as a step to see *if* they want to get married. They enjoy the time together, the access to sex, and being taken care of. In fact, when men get what they want from women, many wonder whether marriage is even necessary.

On the other hand, women tend to view living together as a step *toward* marriage. They tend to view cohabiting as a higher level of commitment than men do. While the nature of marital commitment makes the nature of the relationship clear to everyone, the lack of equal expectations in cohabitation often leads to conflict and disappointment.

Third, the sexual activity that comes with living together can make it harder for spouses to objectively evaluate the relationship. As you will recall, one of the purposes of sex is unity ("become one flesh"). Sex bonds people together spiritually, relationally, and *biochemically*, even if they don't want it to or plan for it to. That premature unity clouds the ability to objectively evaluate the health and viability of a relationship.

Couples sometimes think they can move in together to "test" their compatibility for marriage. What they fail to realize is that the very act of touching one another, being sexually active, and sleeping next to each other triggers the release of oxytocin and creates a powerful bond between them. This chemical bond feels so strong it can blind them to incompatibility in the relationship. Thus, ironically, people move in together to "test the waters," but by doing so, they make it more difficult to be sensible about the wisdom of pursuing marriage.

Here's the bottom line: Living together can make it harder to end an unhealthy relationship. As a result, people who live together *before* marriage are more likely to bring unhealthy patterns *into* their marriage, and thus increase the chances that they will struggle *after* marriage.

Living together can make it harder to end an unhealthy relationship.

After examining decades worth of published academic research, Glenn Stanton concludes, "I cannot think of one way scholars have found in which cohabitation improves a relationship. Its impact is essentially a wholesale negative."[7]

Do you see why God intends couples to leave home, get married, and *then* live together? It is not to limit you, but to bless you in your life and relationships. This pattern will benefit not only you and your future marriage, but also children *and* the rest of society. Once again, we see that God's designs are *for our good* (e.g., Deut. 10:12–13).

Here is my final encouragement: to avoid *sliding* into cohabitation, and thus putting your future marriage at risk, make a *decision* now that you will wait until marriage. If your goal is to work

---

[7] Personal correspondence with me through email on December 12, 2019.

toward a happy, fulfilling, and lasting marriage, this is one of the most important decisions you can make.

>──────→ **QUESTION** ←──────<
What should I do if I become pregnant?

An unexpected pregnancy can be scary. If this is you, the first thing to do is to take a deep breath. Everything is going to be okay. There are caring adults who will walk you through this and help you make the best choice for you and your baby. Do *not* go to a Planned Parenthood clinic. Start by talking to a caring adult, such as your mom or dad, or a youth pastor or Christian teacher. For counseling, direction, and resources, contact a local pregnancy resource center, which can be found through a simple online search.

CHAPTER 25

Divorce

A number of years ago, my wife and I invited a good friend of mine over for dinner so we could spend time with him and his new bride. In the course of the evening, his wife shared how her father—a pastor—had recently divorced her mom and gotten remarried to another woman.

After expressing my regret, I asked her to explain how a pastor could divorce his wife *and still remain a pastor*. "What reasons did he offer?" I asked, in an attempt to understand his biblical justification. And then I pressed her for an answer.

Later that night, after they left, my wife rightly pressed *me* to explain why I had been so rude to our guests. And she was totally right. I was thinking about the issue *biblically* rather than *personally* as a painful situation she was working through. As a professor, sometimes I get lost in the world of *ideas* and forget that we are talking about real *people*! Even though I immediately called her to apologize, I still regret my lack of sensitivity.

When it comes to divorce, we need to be loving toward people *and* we need to look to Scripture as our model. It is a mistake to let our feelings—often formed by a cultural understanding of love—override scriptural truth about marriage and divorce. Yet it is also a mistake to be committed to Scripture, as I was, while lacking graciousness toward others. We need both truth *and* love.

You might say that no one is more pro-divorce before a divorce than Satan, and no one is more anti-divorce after a divorce than Satan. What do I mean by this? Satan would love nothing more than to see countless wrecked marriages leading to countless divorces. He will tempt people with ideas like, *You deserve better, and life will be easier if you end it now.*

But after the divorce, Satan would love nothing more than to trap you in so much shame and guilt that you feel like a second-rate Christian. He'll tempt you with thoughts like, *You're so bad you couldn't even get your marriage to last,* or *Now no one at your church will accept you—better just stay home this Sunday.*

This is not how God sees divorce. God wants to prevent divorce. He does not want marriages to end, and we should avoid divorce at all costs. But when someone has gone through a divorce, they don't need more shame and guilt heaped on them; they need love, grace, and belonging.

The reason we need to be loving is obvious: divorce is painful. It is painful for spouses, kids, friends, and many others. Some of you have experienced this *firsthand.* You know the pain of daily reminders that your mom and dad are no longer committed to each other in marriage.

Given the pain, hurt, and loss that accompanies divorce, it is easy to see why God hates divorce (Mal. 2:16). God wants children to experience the security of knowing their mom and dad love each other and are committed to each other.

As we saw in chapter 19, kids are more likely to thrive physically, academically, and emotionally when they live with their married mom and dad. On the other hand, kids from broken families are more likely to engage in risky behavior, drop out of school, end up in poverty, and experience other negative side effects. The good news, if you're living in one of these families, is that God is in the business of healing wounds, and He wants to give you a new spiritual family. You have felt the harm and hurt of your family crumbling, but you can also taste the joy of being brought into a new family.

As marriages crumble, so does the rest of society. In many ways, the health of a society can be judged by the health of its marriages. God's design for marriage as the permanent union of a man and woman is for the good of children and for the health of the wider society.

There is also a biblical reason why God hates divorce. Marriage is meant to mirror God's loving faithfulness to His people. In the time of the prophets, God called Hosea to marry a prostitute and be faithful to her, as a symbolic act of God's faithfulness to Israel amidst their unfaithfulness to Him. Even though the Israelites lied, stole, killed, and broke the

God's design for marriage as the permanent union of a man and woman is for the good of children and for the health of the wider society.

rest of the Ten Commandments—thus acting as an "adulteress" in their relationship to God—He stayed faithful to them.

Hosea writes, "And the LORD said to me, 'Go again, love a woman who is loved by another man and is an adulteress, even as the LORD loves the children of Israel, though they turn to other gods'" (3:1). Can you imagine that? God actually called the prophet Hosea to *marry a prostitute and be faithful to her even though she would cheat on him,* so the people of Israel could have a visual reminder of God's faithfulness to them.

Of all the potential illustrations available to God, He chose *marriage* as the primary means of portraying His faithfulness to His people. Powerful.

New Testament writers also depict marriage as a mirror for the relationship of God to His people. According to Paul, marriage is a symbol for understanding Christ and His love for the church. He commands husbands to love their wives in the same way Christ sacrificially loved the church (Eph. 5:25). Paul tells us that marriage—which has its roots in the Genesis creation account—points deeply and mysteriously to the relationship between Christ and the church.

This means that if you choose to get married someday, your marriage will be a physical embodiment of God's created design *and* a pointer to the ultimate union of Christ and the church. Marriage is not simply a human construct meant to bring happiness and fulfillment, but a sign of God's unfailing love and commitment to His people. Marriage tells the world the story that when it comes to His people, God is in it for the long haul and He's not going anywhere.

This may sound dramatic, but it's true. If you accept the romantic view of marriage (as we saw in *The Notebook*), you will be tempted to walk away when the emotional intensity drops. But if you understand the higher purpose of marriage, as a pointer to Christ and the church, you will be more likely to stay faithful and committed to your spouse regardless of how you feel.

Holding a biblical view of marriage is vital for marital success.

None of you reading this book plans to get divorced. Honestly, does anyone really go into marriage thinking it will fail? Of course not! People enter marriage with high hopes and dreams. But the reality is that many marriages *do* end in divorce. In fact, while evangelical Christians are more likely to be married than the general population, they are just as likely to experience divorce (25%).[1]

Simply being a Christian will not divorce-proof your future marriage. If you don't think divorce is a possibility in *your* future, you won't take steps *now* to best prevent it. Here are four steps to help divorce-proof your future marriage.

First, *believe that God intends marriage to be permanent.* When Jesus was asked about permissible grounds for divorce, He pointed back to the creation account in Genesis 1–2 and concluded, "What therefore God has joined together, let not man separate" (Matt. 19:6). If marriage was meant to be permanent, His disciples wondered, then why did Moses permit divorce? Jesus responded by indicating that Moses *allowed* divorce because of their "hardness of heart," but that God has always *intended* marriage to be permanent.

Specifically, Jesus permits divorce in cases of sexual immorality (*porneia* in Greek), which refers to a range of sexually immoral behavior such as adultery, homosexual acts, and incest (Matt. 19:9). Some biblical scholars also believe that desertion by a spouse and

---

[1] Barna, "The Trends Redefining Romance Today," (Feb. 9, 2017); https://www.barna.com/research/trends-redefining-romance-today/.

abuse are permissible reasons for divorce (1 Cor. 7:10–15). Here is the point we can't miss: *While Scripture allows divorce for a few reasons, marriage is a covenant before God that is meant to be permanent.*

Second, *realize how deeply your current choices can influence your future marriage.* When couples get engaged, it is easy to justify sexual activity since marriage is coming soon anyway. My wife and I saw some of our friends fall into this trap, so when we were engaged, we were very intentional about maintaining healthy physical boundaries.

While I knew it was the right thing to do, I didn't realize how much this would positively affect my marriage years later. How so? As a speaker and author, I am on the road away from my family quite a bit. Had I pushed physical boundaries *before* marriage, it might be natural for my wife to wonder what boundaries I am pushing *after* marriage. But she doesn't. She trusts me. And a lot of that has to do with the decisions we made physically long before we were married. Preparing for a successful marriage begins with the decisions you are making *now.*

Third, *get to know couples who have healthy marriages.* My father grew up in a severely broken home where there was both sexual abuse and alcoholism. As a result, he didn't have a model of how a man is supposed to love a woman or how a father should love his kids. How did he learn? Simple: he built relationships with healthy married couples. If you have parents who are committed to each other, then take a moment and thank God. There are *millions* of young people who wish they could be like you. If not, then like my father, seek out healthy role models.

Fourth, *plan to seek wise counsel before you get married.* The Bible is full of relational wisdom. Proverbs 11:22 says, "Like a gold ring in a pig's snout is a beautiful woman without discretion." In other words, when you are looking for a spouse, don't sacrifice character for beauty! This wisdom applies to both men and women.

Wise counsel also comes from others. Proverbs 11:14 says, "Where there is no guidance, a people falls, but in an abundance of counselors there is safety."

Please allow me to speak some wise counsel into your life: *If you plan to get married someday, listen to your parents.* No one is more invested in your relational success than your mom and dad (or your closest caregivers). Parents are not perfect, but only a fool would disregard their relational wisdom without serious consideration.

You should also consider the counsel of your fellow church members. We saw earlier how Jesus redefines the family such that our spiritual family is even more vital to our identity than our biological family. Do your fellow church members know your potential spouse? What do they think of him or her? Do they see any red flags?

Marriage is a beautiful union that depicts God's love for the church. If you choose to get married someday, I hope you will experience the joys and blessings of how God has intended marriage to be experienced. And yet rather than following the ideas of our world, I pray you will take the biblical wisdom of this chapter to heart first.

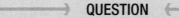

> ⟫───────⟶ **QUESTION** ⟵───────⟪
> *Is it okay to have sex with an animal?*

The Old Testament unequivocally condemns sex with an animal (e.g., Exod. 22:19; Lev. 18:23). While the New Testament does not address bestiality directly, in Romans 1, Paul emphasizes the idolatrous nature of people who have suppressed their knowledge of God, worshipping things in creation rather than the Creator and rejecting God's natural design for sexual relations between male and female. Similar to other forms of sexual immorality, sex with an animal deeply violates God's design for our bodies, and also for how we are to care for animals. Sex with an animal is immoral, unnatural, and degrading to human dignity.

CHAPTER 26

Homosexuality

Not long ago I attended a national conference aimed at reforming the church's historic views on LGBTQ relationships. My goal was simply to meet people and learn about the movement from the inside. Along with worship, testimonies, and lectures, there were multiple in-depth sessions focused on advancing the assertion that the Bible permits modern same-sex relationships. In other words, according to the teachers at this conference, the Bible condemns the kind of homosexual activity that existed in ancient times but permits the kind of LGBTQ relationships we see today.

After the first session, we were split into small groups and sent to classrooms to practice role-playing what we had learned. The teacher started the session by asking each of us to share our stories of why we came to the conference and care so deeply about the movement. Inside I was thinking, *You've got to be kidding me, how did I get myself into this situation? What should I say?*

When it was my turn, I started by mentioning my serious theological reservations about the content at the conference. But then I pulled out the worship packet we were given at registration and read the opening words: "There is love for one like you. There is grace enough to see you through. And wherever you have walked, whatever path you choose, may you know there is love for one like you." I then asked, "We may disagree theologically, but there's a place for me here, right?" At that point they had to say yes, or they would have betrayed their message of inclusion and tolerance.

I expressed my regret that many of them had experienced personal hurt from Christians but also encouraged them not to be tempted to equate disagreement with hate. "The narrative that is often told is that those who don't affirm homosexual behavior are hateful, bigoted, homophobic, and intolerant," I said, "but I want you to know that this is not always true. There are Christians who have serious reservations about your theology but still love you as people."

You may not have been to a conference of this sort, but you have undoubtedly been in a similar situation in which you have felt torn between being committed to biblical truth *and* acting in love. As Christians, we must always be committed to *both*, even if it costs us something.

If you are not same-sex attracted, my hope is that this chapter will equip you to embrace the historic Christian view of sex and marriage—which Jesus held—*and* to live that truth out with a posture of kindness and grace toward others.

If you are a Christian who experiences same-sex attraction, please read these words carefully: *God loves you deeply. You are made in His image and He yearns to be in relationship with you. Please know that God's grace extends to you—yes, you. You are loved. Thank you for trusting me as one voice helping to guide you along your journey of becoming the kind of person God wants you to be.*

Even though they don't get much attention from the wider culture, there are many Christians with same-sex attractions who are staying faithful to the sexual ethic of Jesus. And they are experiencing rich lives.

Consider the story of my friend Christopher Yuan. In 1993, he told his unbelieving parents that he was gay. This announcement completely disrupted his family, to say the least. He embraced "who he was" and went down a path that included promiscuity and illicit drug use. He was eventually expelled from dental school and became a drug supplier.

While his unbelieving mom initially rejected him, when she became a Christian, her heart toward her son changed and she began praying daily that God would bring him to faith in Jesus Christ. After a number of years, God answered her prayers in a dramatic way: Christopher was arrested for drug dealing and went to jail, where he discovered he was HIV positive.

While lying in a jail cell, at the lowest point of his life, he noticed the following words scribbled on the metal bunk: "If you're bored, read Jeremiah 29:11." He not only read this verse but began reading the Bible more and more. In his book *Holy Sexuality and the Gospel*, Christopher writes,

> I realized I'd placed my identity in the wrong thing. The world tells those of us with same-sex attractions that our sexuality is the core of who we are. But God's Word paints quite a different

picture . . . my identity is not gay, ex-gay, or even straight. My *true* identity is in Jesus Christ alone.[1]

Christopher now travels the world with his mom and dad communicating God's grace and truth on biblical sexuality.

Interestingly, when he first became a Christian, a prison chaplain gave Christopher a book claiming that God approves of same-sex relationships. Even though Christopher lacked formal theological training at the time, this message did not ring true with his understanding of Scripture. And his initial instincts were right: *the Bible teaches that God designed sex to be experienced between one man and one woman in marriage.*

Some people today push for a "third way" that allows Christians to "agree to disagree" over the morality of homosexual behavior. Wouldn't this make things easier? After all, the Bible allows for Christians to disagree over a host of important issues (see Rom. 14:1–12). Insofar as the motivation in creating a third way is to make peace among Christians, such a compromise is commendable.

But despite their good intentions, the Bible never considers sexual immorality an agree-to-disagree issue. Scripture speaks of sexual sin with the utmost seriousness. The New Testament includes eight "sin lists" and sexual immorality is included in *all* of them.[2] Specifically, in 1 Corinthians 6:9, Paul lists homosexual acts among the kind of sins that prevent people from inheriting the kingdom

---

[1] Christopher Yuan, *Holy Sexuality and the Gospel: Sex, Desire, and Relationships Shaped by God's Grand Story* (Colorado Springs, CO: Multnomah, 2018), 3.

[2] Mark 7:21–22; Romans 1:28–32; 13:13; 1 Corinthians 6:9–10; Galatians 5:19–21; Colossians 3:5–9; 1 Timothy 1:9–10; Revelation 21:8

of God. This is certainly a controversial view today, but if we truly love people, can we soften the inspired teachings of Scripture?

From the beginning, God designed sex to be experienced within the marital union of one man and one woman (Gen. 1–2). Jesus affirmed this creation account as being normative for human relationships (Matt. 19:3–6). Although He did not mention homosexual behavior explicitly, Jesus affirmed the Old Testament laws about sexual morality, and condemned sexual behavior outside the marriage relationship, which would include homosexual behavior (see Mark 7:21–22).

In Romans 1:21–27, Paul explains that just as turning to idols violates our rightful duty to worship our Creator, so does turning to homosexual relations violate God's natural design for the use of the body as male and female. Some have claimed that Paul was only condemning pederasty, a socially permissible sexual relationship between a man and boy that was prevalent in ancient Greece. However, in this passage, Paul describes the men as performing the *same kind of unnatural practice* as the women, yet there was no female practice of pederasty in ancient Rome. Thus, Paul cannot be speaking about pederasty in Romans 1.

If we truly love people, can we soften the inspired teachings of Scripture?

Others have claimed that Paul was condemning excessive lust, not loving same-sex relationships. In this passage, Paul *does* say that people were "consumed with passion for one another." He does condemn the shameful acts themselves. But why? Because they reflect a denial of the existence of God by violating His clearly seen design for men and women (see 1:18–21). The focus of Romans 1 is not on excessive lust, but on the idolatrous nature of people who have suppressed their knowledge of God, worshipping things in creation rather than the Creator and rejecting God's natural design for sexual relations. As with Jesus, Paul points *back* to creation to ground sexual morality.

Perhaps the most powerful *emotional* argument to affirm same-sex sexual relationships is the claim that historic Christian teaching harms gay people. In reference to the teachings of Jesus about judging a tree by its fruit (Matt. 7:15–20), some claim the "fruit" of historic biblical teaching is harm, and so the teaching itself must be corrected. Sadly, it *is* true that LGBTQ people are more likely to be lonely, depressed, and suicidal. Such a reality should break our hearts and motivate us with compassion toward these people God deeply loves.

But there are two problems with this claim. First, there is no evidence that the traditional teaching *itself* brings harm to LGBTQ people.[3] Many LGBTQ people choose to go to churches that do not affirm same-sex sexual relations because they find meaningful community, vibrant worship, and biblical teaching.

Further, when Jesus says to judge a tree by its fruit, He does not mean that we are free to reject teachings that are emotionally difficult to follow. Rather, according to Jesus, "bad fruit" is teaching that leads people toward disobedience, and "good fruit" is that

---

[3] Mark Yarhouse and Olya Zaporozhets, *Costly Obedience: What We Can Learn from the Celibate Gay Christian Community* (Grand Rapids, MI: Zondervan, 2019), 29–31.

which leads toward repentance and obedience. In the very next two passages, Jesus says "workers of lawlessness" will not enter the kingdom of God, and He says the wise man who builds his house on the rock is the one who "hears these words of mine and does them" (Matt. 7:21–27).

So much more could be said about homosexuality and the Bible. I truly hope you will read more on this topic so you can develop biblical convictions about God's design for sex.[4] In closing, allow me to offer two words of encouragement.

First, *be a good friend.* I recently met a Christian teenage girl who befriended a gay classmate. Rather than feeling the need to begin by telling him he's living in sin; she simply aims to love him as God loves us "while we were still sinners" (Rom. 5:8). They talk, watch movies together, and hang out. Yet when the topic comes up, she graciously shares her beliefs and points to Christ. She certainly hopes he will become a believer, but whether it

True freedom comes not from rejecting the teachings of Jesus, but from embracing the gospel and living in obedience to Christ.

---

[4] If you want to go deeper on the Bible and homosexuality, watch my public conversation with Matthew Vines on YouTube. "What Does the Bible Say about Homosexuality? Sean McDowell and Matthew Vines in Conversation" https://www.youtube.com/watch?v=yFY4VtCWgyI (Feb. 3, 2018). Also check out the book by Christopher Yuan, *Holy Sexuality and the Gospel: Sex, Desire, and Relationships Shaped by God's Grand Story* (Colorado Springs, CO: Multnomah, 2018). Other helpful books on the topic include Sam Allberry's *Is God Anti-Gay?* and Jackie Hill Perry's *Gay Girl, Good God.*

happens or not, she cares about him as a friend, and as an individual made in the image of God. Her approach is to be ready with an answer for her beliefs, and when the time arises, to share them with "gentleness and respect" (1 Pet. 3:15). Who can you reach out to as a friend like this with the love of Jesus?

Second, *stay faithful to Scripture*. Some people today will tell you the Bible approves same-sex sexual relationships. Others will call you a hateful bigot if you embrace God's design for sex and marriage. Don't believe it. As we saw in the example of Christopher Yuan, true freedom comes not from rejecting the teachings of Jesus, but from embracing the gospel and living in obedience to Christ.

My prayer is that this faithfulness will characterize *you*.

≫———→ QUESTION ←———≪
What should I do if a friend comes out to me?

If a friend comes out to you, the first thing to do is to be thankful you have a friend who cares enough to share this part of their journey with you. Since people are often very vulnerable when they come out, be sure to communicate that you care about the person *no matter what*. Listen, empathize, and ask genuine questions about how they are doing and how you can help now and in the future. Avoid theological discussions about morality—there will be a time for that, but it isn't the moment a person comes out. For now, show your love and care for the person.

CHAPTER 27

Same-Sex Marriage

Not too long ago, I was invited to speak at a prestigious Christian high school in Southern California. Instead of giving a lecture, I decided to engage the students in conversation to see how well they could articulate a biblical view of sex and marriage *without using the Bible*. I began by offering a case for same-sex marriage and inviting the students to respond. After merely three minutes of near silence, one twelfth grade girl, who looked both frustrated and anxious, blurted out, "Dr. McDowell, I really want to be able to affirm a biblical view of marriage, but I have no idea how. Where do I start?"

In my experience, this girl expressed the frustration many young Christians feel today. They want to be able to affirm in both their words and actions the biblical view of marriage that has been held by the church for two thousand years but lack the ability to do so.

In this chapter, my goal is to teach you how to make a case for the biblical view of marriage—which I will call "natural marriage"—without using the Bible. We have seen that God has designed marriage as a permanent, lifelong commitment between a man and a woman (Gen. 1, 2). The Bible presents *this* view of marriage as true not only for Christians but for all of humanity. Since God has built natural marriage into the fabric of reality, we can make a reasonable case for the biblical view *without relying upon Scripture*.

Remember, God has designed marriage *for our good*. He designed marriage to mirror His love for the church *and* to benefit mankind. Thus, children suffer when they don't have the benefit of a committed mother and father. We see this in the lives of many people who grow up with same-sex parents.

Consider the story of Millie Fontana, a young atheist from Melbourne.[1] The narrative is that kids of same-sex parents are well-loved, stable, and happy. The reason for this narrative, according to Millie, is the LGBTQ ideology that kids don't need a mom and dad, and that "love is love." Yet this was *not* her experience growing up.

"The truth," says Millie, "is that growing up with two mothers forced me to be confused about who I was and where I fit in the scheme of the world." Father's Day was particularly difficult. She was told, "You have another mother," as if that was supposed to console her. She not only felt a deep yearning for her father, but she *also* felt guilty for feeling as if she rejected her other mom when she shared her experience.

If we set aside political correctness for a moment, claims Millie, we see that same-sex marriage puts adult *desires* above the *needs* of children. Millie says that while both straight and gay relationships should be respected, "We cannot say 'yes' to homosexual marriage

---

[1] Millie Fontana, "Growing up with two mothers forced me to be confused about who I was and where I fit in the scheme of the world" (April 11, 2017); https://thembeforeus.com/millie-fontana/.

without invalidating a child's right to both genders." According to Millie, "marriage equality" is not about equality for children, but equality for adults.

Millie is not alone in her experience. Even though many face rejection and discrimination, dozens of kids with same-sex parents have been willing to share the heartbreaking part of their stories.[2] I encourage you to explore the stories and see for yourself.

Here is the bottom line: while kids who grow up with same-sex parents often feel loved, they are always missing either the maternal or paternal love that they crave. Kids with two moms often *yearn* for a relationship with their father. Kids with two dads *yearn* for a relationship with their mother. And they also desire the security that comes from having a mom and dad who love each other. Yet each of these desires is negated by the very nature of their family.

It is vital for people to hear stories like that of Millie Fontana, for they rarely get a voice in our larger culture. But we also need to offer good arguments for why we embrace natural marriage, and to do so with "gentleness and respect" (1 Pet. 3:15).

While kids who grow up with same-sex parents often feel loved, they are always missing either the maternal or paternal love that they crave.

---

[2] For a list, see Them Before Us; https://thembeforeus.com/tag/lgbt -parents/page/4/.

According to Maggie Gallagher, there are three obviously true facts about the world that make the institution of marriage necessary. Unsurprisingly, these three facts align with the biblical view of marriage.

First, *sex makes babies*. This should be obvious. And it is. But we have to state it because proponents of the sexual revolution have worked hard to separate sex and babies in the minds of people today.

Because of birth control (and especially the pill) as well as abortion, many people have been conditioned to think that sex is not about making babies. Yet by its very nature, sex is a procreative act. Sure, babies do not result every time. Sometimes the creation of babies is prevented when people use contraception. Nevertheless, even despite our technological advances, babies are the natural result of sexual activity between a man and a woman. *Sex makes babies*.

Second, *society needs babies*. Considering that the mortality rate is 100 percent, society needs replacements. To survive, civilizations must care about the process that produces children, which is why every society has a vested interest in sex. Currently, many countries around the world are experiencing a demographic crisis because people are not having enough babies. In Japan, for instance, the fertility rate is 1.41, which is why experts forecast a "severe economic downturn and a breakdown in the fabric of social life."[3] If they want to survive, *societies need babies*.

---

[3] Chris Weller, "'This is death to the family': Japan's fertility crisis is creating economic and social woes never seen before," *Business Insider* (May 21, 2017); https://www.businessinsider.com/japan-fertility-crisis-2017-4. The rate is measured as 1.41 children to every one woman, or couple.

In his dissenting opinion to the *Obergefell v. Hodges* (2015) Supreme Court ruling that sanctioned same-sex marriage into law, Chief Justice John Roberts said:

> The human race must procreate to survive. Procreation occurs through sexual relations between a man and a woman. When sexual relations result in the conception of a child, that child's prospects are generally better if the mother and father stay together rather than going their separate ways. Therefore, for the good of children and society, sexual relations that can lead to procreation should occur only between a man and a woman committed to a lasting bond. Society has recognized that bond as marriage.[4]

Do you notice the structure of his argument? He notes that sex makes babies ("procreation occurs through sexual relations between a man and a woman"), which is our first point. He also notes that society needs babies ("the human race must procreate to survive"), which is our second point. And then Roberts makes Gallagher's third point.

Babies need a mom and a dad ("the child's prospects are generally better if the mother and father stay together"). This is the very reason why the government is involved in legally binding a man and woman together through marriage in the first place—it's because the *opposite-sex union* is the kind of union that makes

---

[4] The dissent by Justice John Roberts (2015), 5; https://www.supreme court.gov/opinions/14pdf/14-556_3204.pdf.

babies, and those babies need a stable family, a family with both a mother and a father.

Since the 1970s, dozens of studies have attempted to assess the effects of same-sex relations on children. There has been a general "no difference" consensus, which holds that children of same-sex unions fare just as well as children with opposite-sex parents (and sometimes better). Yet, the evidence does not support this claim. In his massive analysis of the research on same-sex parenting, Walter Schumm concludes that the preliminary evidence weighs against the claim that gender is irrelevant for child well-being.[5]

The loving position is support of natural marriage, for that is the institution that is *truly best* for kids.

In reality, mothers and fathers parent differently, and both matter for the healthy development of kids. Mothers tend to be more verbal and nurturing with their kids, and fathers tend to be more action-oriented and demanding.[6] Honestly, doesn't this ring true to you? In your own family, as well as the families of your friends, isn't it obvious that men and women parent differently? Studies and common sense both reveal that *babies need a mom and a dad.*

---

[5] Walter R. Schumm, "A Review and Critique of Research on Same-Sex Parenting and Adoption," *Psychological Reports*, Vol. 119, No. 3 (Sept. 12, 2016), 656.

[6] Scott Haltzman, "The Effect of Gender-Based Parental Influences on Raising Children," in *Gender and Parenthood: Biological and Scientific Perspectives*, ed. W. Bradford Wilcox & Kathleen Kovner Kline (New York: Columbia University Press, 2013), 318.

In sum, here is our simple case: (1) Sex makes babies, (2) Society needs babies, and (3) Babies need a mom and a dad.

If these three points are true, despite protestations to the contrary, the loving position is support of natural marriage, for that is the institution that is *truly best* for kids.

What can you do? The focus of this book has been about loving God and loving others. In terms of marriage, here are seven things *you* can do to help create a healthy marriage culture, which benefits *everyone*:

- Pray for the married, engaged, and dating couples you know.
- Consider becoming a marriage counselor to help spouses mend broken marriages.
- Learn the art of filmmaking or writing so you can tell compelling stories about the goodness and beauty of natural marriage.
- Study law so you can legally defend the religious liberty of people who believe that marriage is between a man and a woman.
- Be willing to have conversations with people about marriage with gentleness and respect.
- Build friendships with students who have same-sex parents so they can see that you *and* God deeply love them.

Ultimately, if you want to get married someday, commit to becoming the kind of spouse and parent God desires for you to be so that your marriage can be a testimony of God's faithfulness to your generation.

⟫———————➤ **QUESTION** ⟵———————⟪
Can you be gay and Christian?

This depends on what we mean by "gay." Can a Christian experience same-sex attraction? Of course. Can a Christian commit sexual sin, including homosexual behavior, and be forgiven? Absolutely. Can a person engage in unrepentant same-sex sexual behavior and be a Christian? That's tougher. The Bible is clear that sex is meant for one man and one woman in marriage. And it places homosexual behavior in the category of sins that keeps someone from inheriting the kingdom of God (1 Cor. 6:9–11).

CHAPTER 28

Transgender

When the Supreme Court was about to decide on the issue of same-sex marriage, I got a call from a producer at CNN asking if I would be on a panel to discuss the ruling at their Los Angeles studio. Since my wife was hanging with some friends that night, and I was in charge of our three kids, I had to decline.

Shortly thereafter, the producer called me back asking if I would be a call-in guest to discuss the gender transition of Bruce Jenner, a former U.S. Olympian, to Caitlin Jenner. I agreed, and he asked me to briefly share my views. As best I can remember, I said the following:

> Jesus loves transgender people. This issue has become too political. The research shows that transgender people are more likely to suffer with loneliness, depression, and suicide than the general population. Thus, we need to reach across the political aisle and find common ground with others for the sake of helping men and women who are transgender.

After a long silence, he finally spoke. And I will never forget what he said: "I am sorry. I can't have you on the show. You are much too compassionate."

In retrospect, I should have anticipated his response. I was naïve enough to think they actually wanted to help transgender people. Watching the show that night, and seeing how chaotic and divisive it was, confirmed my suspicions that they were more interested in ratings (and pushing a particular agenda) than in truly helping people who are transgender.

Our society is undergoing a gender revolution. Girl. Boy. Woman. Man. Sex. Gender. In the minds of an increasing number of people today—and especially *young* people—these words no longer mean what they used to mean.

Thus, it will be helpful to begin with some definitions.

- **Transgender** refers to a person who experiences incongruence between his or her biological sex and his or her gender identity. Many transgender people describe their *experience* as feeling trapped in the wrong body.
- **Gender dysphoria** describes the psychological distress that some transgender people experience. While most people with gender dysphoria identify as transgender, some don't. And not all transgender people experience gender dysphoria. Transgender is used as an identity; gender dysphoria is a *psychological condition*.
- People who are **intersex** experience atypical development of their sexual anatomy and/

or sex chromosomes. In a minor number of cases, some individuals have both XX and XY chromosomes, which can lead to the development of both male and female sex organs. Unlike transgender, intersex is a *biological condition.*

- **Transgenderism** is an *ideology* that aims to transform cultural understandings of sex and gender. The goal is to uproot the idea that humans are naturally sexed beings and to move society away from being shaped by the gender binary. Transgenderism is being pushed in the media—as evidenced in my CNN story—as well as the educational system,[1] legal system, Hollywood, some churches, and so on.

Interestingly, it is not merely Christians who question transgender ideology. There are *many* lesbians, feminists, and medical professionals who are opposed to transgender ideology. A number of transsexuals—who have had sex-change surgery—are even opposed to it.[2]

---

[1] In California, parents can opt their kids out of sexual health education, but not out of gender education. Starting in kindergarten, kids are taught to embrace transgender ideology. See Sean McDowell, "New California Health Standards Lack Diversity, Inclusion, and Openness," (Feb. 14, 2019); https://seanmcdowell.org/blog/new-california-health-standards-lack-diversity-inclusion-and-openness.

[2] Consider watching a few YouTube videos of their stories: Corinna: https://youtu.be/5pm-W0r-Xwo, Lady Boi: https://youtu.be/bd3TjU-credo, Rose of Dawn: https://youtu.be/hf_Ajljavy4, Kinesis: https://youtu.

Recently, a group of psychologists, philosophers, social workers, and feminists from the UK and USA contributed to the academic book *Transgender Children and Young People: Born in Your Own Body*,[3] which critiques the transgender movement. Not only is this group not attempting to promote a Christian perspective, but one of the writers even makes it clear that he considers Christians bigots.[4]

Yet, the editors of the book concluded that "in the guise of offering a new paradigm of thought and a revolution in values, transgendering children is not progressive, but politically reactionary, medically dangerous and abusive of children."[5] Strong words.

Motivated to protect kids from harm, the scholars make a few scientifically supportable observations:

- A high percentage of children who identify as transgender exhibit autism traits (one study indicates 50 percent).

- Telling children that their "real selves" can be disassociated from their bodies teaches them

be/2QJMSw5HnWU, Jadis Argiope: https://youtu.be/vIxXD6a7xv0, and Kalvin Garrah: https://youtu.be/N5VCS0SOuMg.

[3] Heather Brunskell-Evans and Michele Moore, eds. *Transgender Children and Young People: Born in Your Own Body* (Newcastle, UK: Cambridge Scholars Press, 2018), 3.

[4] The anonymous "Gender Critical Dad" writes, "Or worse, am I thinking like a religious bigot, who really hates people who aren't heterosexual because they think it says to do so in the Bible?" GenderCriticalDad, "I'm Not a Hideously Bigoted Parent Who Doesn't 'Get it,'" in *Transgender Children and Young People*, 67.

[5] Heather Brunskell-Evans and Michele Moore, eds. *Transgender Children and Young People: Born in Your Own Body*, 3.

to accept a mind-body split, which is a form of psychological "dis-ease."

- The stories of detransitioners undermines the claim that transgender surgery is an effective treatment for gender dysphoria.[6] In fact, studies do not support the claim that sex-reassignment surgery helps transgender people, as a whole, have better psychological outcomes.[7]

Ultimately, how you process the transgender question depends on your worldview. From a Christian perspective, there are three important biblical truths to remember.[8] First, as we have seen, God made humans in His image as male and female (Gen. 1:27). Thus, humans are intrinsically sexed beings.

Second, the Bible consistently condemns crossing gender boundaries (Deut. 22:5). We are called to love God with our bodies *and* our souls in congruence.

Third, Scripture isn't very specific about what it means to live out one's biological sex. Thus, gender expression varies quite considerably across cultures of the world. Also, as Christians, we need to be especially careful not to import gender stereotypes into our relationships. When we define gender boxes too rigidly, we make it

---

[6] For a range of stories of people who regret undergoing a sex change, see sexchangeregret.com.

[7] See Lawrence S. Mayer and Paul R. McHugh, "Sexuality and Gender: Findings from the Biological, Psychological, and Social Sciences," in *The New Atlantis*, No. 50 (Fall 2016), 111.

[8] I am deeply indebted to Preston Sprinkle for this section. See Preston Sprinkle, "Pastoral Paper: A Biblical Conversation about Transgender Identities," www.centerforfaith.com.

easy for people who do not fit the stereotypes to consider joining the other gender.

When I ask Christian audiences who they consider a "manly man" in the Bible, most mention King David. Was he acting manly when he killed Goliath? All agree. But what about when he played a harp and wrote poetry? Scripture offers no hint that these were feminine actions. David was both a warrior *and* a poet.[9]

Does this mean there are no significant differences between boys and girls? No! In fact, gender is so important for how children learn, Dr. Leonard Sax notes, that "trying to understand a child without understanding the role of gender in child development is like trying to understand a child's behavior without knowing the child's age."[10] In fact, he considers gender to be more revealing for how a child learns than age.

Consider a few key differences Dr. Sax observes between males and females:

- The average girl hears and smells better than the average boy.
- When given paper and crayons, girls tend to draw flowers and trees with lots of colors. Boys are more likely to draw action scenes, such as with monsters and aliens.

---

[9] Again, my thanks to Preston Sprinkle for this observation.
[10] Leonard Sax, *Why Gender Matters: What Parents and Teachers Need to Know about the Emerging Science of Sex Differences* (New York, NY: Harmony Books, 2017), 8.

- After fighting, boys are more likely to become better friends. With girls, hurt feelings often linger.
- Young men tend to be interested in sex for the sake of sex, whereas young women are more likely to desire sex in the context of a committed relationship. And this is true regardless of whether someone has opposite-sex or same-sex sexual attractions.

This list is only the tip of the iceberg. According to Dr. Sax, gender differences extend to school motivation, drug and alcohol use, engagement in social media, and more. The bottom line is that science is revealing significant gender differences that emerge *early* in childhood development. Failing to recognize these differences, says Sax, brings significant harm to children.

Science is revealing significant gender differences that emerge *early* in childhood development.

Yet it is also important to recognize that these are statistical *averages*. Some males and females fall outside the general pattern, and yet *they are still male or female* based on their biology. For instance, if a female is interested in "sex for the sake of sex," she's still female, even if most females don't experience sexual desire in that way. Likewise, if a young boy likes drawing colorful pictures of trees and flowers, he's still male.

So how are we to respond? We need young Christians to become pastors who will help people struggling with gender dysphoria. We need young Christians to become politicians and lawyers who will defend the rights of people who want the freedom to live their lives, and run their businesses, according to their convictions about marriage. We need young Christians to become psychologists, philosophers, and sociologists with the courage to do quality research demonstrating the reality of sex differences. And we need young people to become communicators who use social media to help advance a Christian worldview.

In other words, we need young people to resist destructive ideologies and to take a stand against unbiblical and unscientific ideas about the fundamentals of human nature. Could this be *you*?

These steps may be down the road for you. For now, please allow me to offer three action steps you can take to better love transgender people:

First, *be motivated by compassion*. Gender dysphoria is a deep, painful struggle that often results in tears and anguish. According to one study, 41 percent of transgender men and women attempt suicide, which is shocking when compared to the national average of 1.6 percent. My prayer is that God will give you a heart of compassion for this group of people God dearly loves.

Second, *be quick to listen and slow to speak*. James, the brother of Jesus, said to be "quick to hear, slow to speak" (James 1:19). Rather than look to "fix" people who are transgender, focus on being a good listener. Ask questions and show sincere interest in their life experiences. Listen. Listen. Listen. Be a good friend.

Third, *speak truth compassionately*. Our culture promotes gender confusion. It punishes those who stray from the transgender narrative. Yet, like the apostles of Jesus, we should be more concerned with obeying God than with satisfying the opinions of men (Acts 4:18–20; 5:29). Be bold. Speak truth. But do so with an extra dose of compassion and kindness, knowing that transgender people—as all people—only experience freedom through embracing God's design for their lives.

⟫————→ QUESTION ←————⟪
Is it okay for a Christian to pursue transgender surgery?

Scripture says God designed people as male and female. Biological sex is thus essential to being human. Scripture also says humans have been made as body *and* soul, and that our bodies are part of God's good creation. Since our bodies are part of the identity God has assigned us, we are called to express our gender in a way that matches who we are. Scripture does not give permission for identifying as a sex or gender in opposition to our biological sex, which would include pursuing transgender surgery. Additionally, there is a lack of convincing scientific evidence that sex transition surgery helps patients. Therefore, it is not okay for a Christian to pursue gender reassignment surgery.

CHAPTER 29

Sexual Abuse

My father is my hero. One of the big reasons for this is what he has overcome in his life. From ages six to thirteen, he was severely sexually abused by a man who lived on his family's farm in Union City, Michigan. One of the darkest days of his life was when he told his mother (my grandmother), but she refused to listen. After all, people didn't talk about sexual abuse much in the 1950s.

To protect himself, he would get in trouble at school in order to be disciplined and forced to stay at school late into the afternoon. The abuse only stopped when, as a thirteen-year old, he was strong enough to slam the man against the wall and threaten him.

If you are a victim of sexual abuse, you know exactly what my father went through. The loneliness, shame, and powerlessness can be debilitating. In her book aimed at helping the church respond to the current sex abuse crisis, sex abuse survivor Mary DeMuth says, "I can think of no other crime, other than murder, that leaves a human more damaged and broken than sexual abuse.

Its long-lasting trauma causes survivors to question the goodness of God."[1]

The harm of sex abuse runs deep.

Sex abuse harms people *physically*. In research for his book *Healing the Wounded Heart*, Dan Allender asked members of a recovery group how past abuse affected their present health. Many were able to identify physical ailments that traced back to their abuse from years earlier. The stress from sex abuse, says Allender, leaves the body of a survivor "vulnerable, susceptible, and fragile long after the abuse has ended."[2]

Sex abuse also harms people *spiritually*. Those who have experienced sexual abuse are more likely to feel lonely, jaded, depressed, and even suicidal. Many abuse survivors find themselves wondering why God, if He is truly loving, could allow such a horrible thing to happen to them. These feelings are understandable, to say the least.

If you have been sexually abused, please allow me to speak these words from my heart:

> *I am so sorry. My heart breaks for what was done to you. It was not your fault. By God's grace, many other sex abuse survivors, including my father, have experienced healing and freedom. I pray this chapter will be one part of your longer journey to transformation.*

If you have not been sexually abused, I pray this chapter will help you be more educated and compassionate toward those who

---

[1] Mary DeMuth, *We Too: How the Church Can Respond Redemptively to the Sexual Abuse Crisis* (Eugene, OR: Harvest House, 2019), 116.

[2] Dan B. Allender, *Healing the Wounded Heart* (Grand Rapids, MI: Baker, 2016), 61.

have been. The problem is real. And it's big. With the ubiquity of pornography and the proliferation of sex trafficking, sex abuse has become a massive issue today. We must *all* be ready to respond with love and truth.

So, what is sexual abuse? According to Dr. Kathryn-Scott Young, "Sexual abuse is one person's misuse of power over another person in a sexual manner."[3] There are different kinds of sexual abuse that range from sexual innuendos, being forced to watch pornography, being touched inappropriately, to rape. While these actions can often have different effects on a victim, it is vital to realize that *abuse is abuse*. No matter where it falls on the spectrum, all sexual abuse is harmful and wrong.

Despite the pervasive cultural assumption, males are not the only ones who sexually abuse boys. While perpetrators are likely to be male, sexual abuse by women is more common than previously thought. And perpetrators are typically not strangers, but someone known to the victim.

Why is the damage of sexual abuse so difficult to discuss? The answer is simple, yet powerful: *Satan is crafty.* Remember, God designed sex to be a beautiful experience between husband and wife. Sex is part of God's good creation! Satan hates the joyful pleasure of sex and, as a murderer, he is committed to destroying life. He wants sexual abuse survivors to feel too ashamed to share their experiences. While the #MeToo movement has helped empower people to open up, the church still has a long way to go to overcome the toxic shame many survivors experience. Satan's strategy is

---

[3] Kathryn Scott-Young, "Sexual Abuse," in *The Popular Encyclopedia of Christian Counseling*, ed. Dr. Tim Clinton and Dr. Ron Hawkins (Eugene, OR: Harvest House, 2011), 303.

simple: propagate lies about sex in general, and sex abuse victims in particular, so they will be silenced and shamed.

Thus, understanding how God views sexual abuse is part of the road to freedom. Scripture reveals three important points:

First, *the Bible is honest about sex abuse*. The Bible speaks openly and honestly about sexual abuse. Consider a couple examples. In the sad epoch of Sodom and Gomorrah, Lot offers his daughters to a group of men who want to rape his guests. Both cities are destroyed for their wickedness (Gen. 19). King David, who is called "a man after God's own heart," uses his power as king to have sex with Bathsheba and then murder her husband to hide his guilt. David may have loved the Lord, but he committed a grave act of sexual exploitation against Bathsheba. The Bible does not hide the reality of sexual abuse, even from its heroes.

Second, *God has a heart for the marginalized*. While the nation of Israel was expected to care for those who were disenfranchised, we see God's heart for the marginalized fully expressed in Jesus. He cared for those with disabilities, the poor, the sick, the demon-possessed, lepers, and others who were considered outcasts from society. In terms of the marginalized, women were particularly drawn to Jesus. They adored Him. They longed to touch Him, to serve Him, and to pour perfume on Him. And yet unlike the founders of other religions, such as Muhammed, Joseph Smith,

God has a heart for the marginalized.

Charles Taze Russell, and Gautama Buddha, Jesus treated women with the highest dignity, kindness, and respect.[4]

Finally, *Jesus understands*. God is not distant from our suffering. In the person of Jesus, God took on human flesh and experienced the full weight of temptation yet remained sinless (see Heb. 4:15). God knows what it's like to be misunderstood, betrayed, mocked, beaten, *and* humiliated. He was stripped naked and crucified publicly. While the Bible does not report that Jesus was sexually abused, we can be confident that He empathizes profoundly with the shame that survivors often feel. As Mary DeMuth explains, "Our beautiful, empathetic Savior understands what it's like to live in this violent, sexually charged world. He knows betrayal and physical pain."[5]

If you were sexually abused, Jesus hurts with *you*.

In particular, here are three points of encouragement for those who have experienced sexual abuse:

Recognize your identity in Christ. I recently asked my dad how he became a healthy person in light of his experience with sexual abuse. His response caught me off guard: "Son, I chose not to see myself as used goods." In other words, while he could not control what that evil man did to him, he could control how he responded. As difficult as it was, he came to embrace the belief that his value transcended the abuse. As he became a Christian, he understood more deeply that his value came from his relationship with Christ (2 Cor. 5:17). You too are not defined by what happened to you.

---

[4] See Jonalyn Fincher, "Defending Femininity: Why Jesus is Good News for Women," in *Apologetics for a New Generation*, ed., Sean McDowell (Eugene, OR: Harvest House, 2009), 222–29.

[5] DeMuth, *We Too*, 46.

God says you are a beautiful, wonderful creation and that He yearns to be in relationship with you.

Second, *share your experience with someone*. This can be a scary step, but it is vital for beginning the journey of healing from sexual abuse. People didn't talk about sexual abuse much when my father was younger, but now they do. Teachers, counselors, pastors, and others are poised to believe *your* story and help you overcome it. It is understandable that you would feel fear and shame for sharing your story. But the only way to begin the journey of healing is to open up and share with a trusted adult.

Third, *speak out with your story*. I hesitate to share this point, because I don't want to move too quickly over the hurt and pain of sexual abuse. Dealing with sexual abuse is a journey that often takes a lifetime. Yet many courageous sexual abuse survivors have shared their stories publicly and experienced the power of helping others. My friend Lisa Michelle, for instance, is a survivor of sexual exploitation. Her story is heartbreaking and yet also a testimony of how God can transform the most broken lives. I hope you will listen to it.[6] She is now a speaker and the founder of No Strings Attached Ministries, which reaches out to women who work in the sex industry.

If you have been sexually abused, my prayer is that God will bring the right people into your life so you can get the healing that you need. And when the time is right, that He will equip you to

---

[6] "Surviving Sexual Abuse and Exploitation (with Lisa Michelle)," an episode of the *Think Biblically Podcast*, cohosted by Sean McDowell and Scott Rae; https://www.biola.edu/blogs/think-biblically/2019/surviving-sexual-abuse-and-exploitation (January 10, 2019).

share your story with others, so you can see how your life can bring hope to others.

What about those who haven't been sexually abused? What can you do to help? First and foremost, we need Christians to embody a biblical sexual ethic and disciple others who will. In a sexualized, pornified world, as we have already seen, we—especially young men—are trained to view other people as sexual objects. The journey from viewing someone as a sexual object to sexually abusing them is not a long one. We need to embody the sexual ethic of Jesus, who saw every human being as a man or woman bearing the image of God, and thus worthy of dignity, value, respect, and love. And we need to disciple others to do the same.

We also need young Christians to become counselors to help people overcome the crippling effects of sex abuse. We need young Christians to work with organizations such as the International Justice Mission that aim to end worldwide slavery, including sex slavery. We need young Christians to become filmmakers to capture the horror of sex abuse and tell powerful stories of redemption. We need young Christians to be good listeners to those who have experienced sex abuse.

Could this be *you*?

QUESTION

What do I do if someone tells me they are being sexually abused?

If someone tells you they are being sexually abused, be thankful that the person trusts you enough to share this intimate part of their life, and that you can now help him or her. Rather than freaking out, simply respond by listening empathetically and being a good friend. Tell your friend you love them and will stand by them no matter what. It is also vital that this information be shared with the proper authorities. Sexual abuse isn't just personally harmful and evil; it is illegal, and you are required to notify the proper authorities. You can offer to go with your friend to tell an adult, but you also need to ensure legal authorities are notified. For this, you can call the National Sexual Assault Telephone Hotline (800-656-4673) or the local police.

CHAPTER 30

You Can Do It!

If you have made it this far in the book, you might be thinking, *This seems impossible. How can I possibly remain sexually pure in our sex-saturated world?* These feelings are totally understandable. Trust me, I have been there.

Yet here is the bottom line: You *can* do it. Yes, *you* can follow God's design for sex, love, and relationships starting today.

My point is not that you can be perfect. Perfection is an impossible standard to aim for and will set you up for discouragement, shame, and failure.

But if we focus on trusting God and His grace amidst our daily struggles, and understand that forgiveness and growth are part of the process, *then* we can follow God's design for sex, love, and relationships.

How can I say this so confidently? For one, many young people *are* following God's plan for sex and relationships. I regularly meet thousands of teens around the world who are aiming to live countercultural lives in obedience to Christ. They are resisting the cultural narrative about sex and trusting God to guide their relationships.

Do they fall short at times? Yes. Is it always easy? No. But remember, as we saw in the early part of this book, doing difficult things is meaningful. Nothing worth having comes easy. You *can* join the movement of young people choosing to live their lives in obedience to Christ.

Second, I did it. Even though my wife and I dated nearly ten years, we were not sexually active until we got married. Does that mean I was perfect? Of course not. Like everyone else, I have made plenty of mistakes in my life. But the older I get, the more grateful I am that my parents helped me build convictions about God's design for relationships.

You might be thinking, *but times were different then.* Fair enough. I grew up in the 80s and early 90s. While social media had not yet been invented, there was porn, peer pressure, and sexually explicit music and movies. While my wife and I were not sexually active, there were certainly times I wondered if it was worth it. After all, some of my friends seemed to be having a lot of fun and experiencing minimal consequences. Was God's plan really best?

God can be trusted.

The older I get, the more thankful I am that my parents instilled in me a sense that God's plan *is* best. They taught me that God can be trusted. They taught me that God gives us commands for our good. They taught me that true freedom comes from living faithfully before God. And they taught me that when I make a mistake, God is quick to forgive.

I am personally experiencing many blessings as a result of taking this message to heart, and I hope that will be your experience too.

Finally, according to the apostle Paul, we *do* have the power to resist temptation: "No temptation has overtaken you that is not common to man. God is faithful, and he will not let you be tempted beyond your ability, but with the temptation he will also provide the way of escape, that you may be able to endure it" (1 Cor. 10:13). In other words, God is the one, through the power of the Holy Spirit, and the love of other Christians, who enables us to live faithfully. You have the God of the universe on your side.

Using an illustration from *The Matrix*, I began this book by asking a general question about which path you will choose: the pleasure-filled life focused on self-fulfillment or the path of giving your life away for a greater cause? In other words, will you accept the invitation of the world or the invitation of Jesus?

The contrast could not be starker. So much is at stake. You can't stay on the sidelines. And you can't serve two masters. Closing this book and ignoring the question *is a choice*.

So, what will it be? What will *you* choose?

QUESTION

Is remaining sexually pure an unrealistic goal today?

Given our sexually infatuated culture, is it difficult to remain sexually pure today? Yes. Can being sexually pure cause you to be treated differently than others? Possibly. But is it unrealistic? *No!* Many young people today are choosing not to be sexually active. You are not an animal who acts entirely on instinct. You are a human being, made in the image of God, who is free to love, think, and make moral choices. Anyone who tells you it is unrealistic to wait for marriage is lying. Many young people are choosing to remain sexually pure. By God's grace *you* can too.

Also available
from
Sean McDowell

How do we seek God and His kingdom first in our relationships with other people? This is the great task Jesus has called us to.

New 9-Session Bible Study for Teens available wherever Bible studies are sold